To EMILY MOORE

FOR THREE REASONS

FIRSTLY—*Because she is a very charming old lady.*

SECONDLY—*Because for 40 years she was the hostess of that old Coaching House, the Swan Inn, at Leatherhead.*

AND LASTLY—*That many, many years ago she befriended and gave to a very shy and very red-headed youth his first commission; the result of which was the terribly bad picture which now hangs in her dining-room.*

The
ROMANCE
of the ROAD

A COACHING INN

WRITTEN AND ILLUSTRATED BY

CECIL ALDIN

BRACKEN BOOKS
LONDON

FIRST PUBLISHED BY EYRE & SPOTTISWOODE IN 1928

THIS EDITION PUBLISHED 1986 BY
BRACKEN BOOKS A DIVISION OF BESTSELLER PUBLICATIONS LTD
BRENT HOUSE, 24 FRIERN PARK, NORTH FINCHLEY, LONDON

ISBN 1 85170 001 3

PRINTED AND BOUND IN GREAT BRITAIN
BY CLARK CONSTABLE, EDINBURGH AND LONDON

LIST OF COLOUR PLATES

AND THIS IS THE STORY OF SOME OF ITS INNS, ROADS, COACHES, AND TRAVELLERS

IN eighteen hundred and twenty-eight, when the coaching age was at its zenith, and when, instead of petrol pumps and advertisement hoardings, horses, coachmen, and inns had the limelight, Patterson's road map and coaching time-table was the traveller's guide, philosopher, and friend. On this map, with its mail-coach roads clearly marked, we saw a picture which resembled a giant octopus, whose ever-twisting tentacles spread in every direction over the landscape.

Then the map of England represented a beautiful thing, instead of the series of architecturally ruled lines which our cartographers will produce a few years hence, picturing, as they will do, the great straight arterial motor and by-pass roads: a map representing something very similar to the straight ruled lines on the face of a sundial.

On these mail-coach roads, instead of the skating-rink surface of to-day, we had a highway of good, sound macadam; and, above all, we had a varied and delightful landscape and vista ahead of us, instead of, as we so often see now, a road with every bend, corner, and tree carefully eliminated.

In two thousand and twenty-eight the countryside will probably be a mass of hoardings, petrol pumps, and aeroplane landing-stations—a cross between the view we now get when travelling upon the railway between Birmingham and Wolverhampton, or motoring out of London on the ugly Great West Road.

But two thousand and twenty-eight is as much ahead of our own times as eighteen hundred and twenty-eight is behind them, and as contemplation of the picturesque past is more pleasant than speculation on the ugly future, we will return to the King's highway of 1828, to the rattle of the bars and pole-chains of the coaches, and forget for one brief hour that we have ever seen a railway train, motor-bus, telephone, telegraph pole, wireless aerial, aeroplane, or Douglas Fairbanks and Mary Pickford.

In these preliminary pages, and before we set out on our journeys, I should like you to visualize the people we may meet, the roads we may travel over, the carriages we may ride in, and the inns we shall pass, in the dress, features, build, and architectural adornments in which they appeared in the year of my story. Therefore I put before you this introductory puppet-show-prologue in which we will take a first view of some of my actors and properties.

Some of us remember the old-time showman (the precursor of our Charles B. Cochran and Bertram Mills) who stood outside his booth before the performance commenced, thumping on his drum and declaiming of the wonders within.

THE SHOWMAN.

We remember also how a few of his star performers would be paraded in full grease-paint (and, unfortunately for them, in the cold daylight) before the crowd, or otherwise, waiting to enter his show.

Like this old-time showman, my puppets shall also make a first appearance on the threshold of my booth, in order, I hope, to persuade you to enter.

My characters and properties, however, will not be dressed up to act a part, but, to me at any rate, will be the real travellers, coaches, inns, and roads of 1828, all being evolved from prints and paintings which were drawn from life at the actual period which they depict.

An orchestration of atmosphere played before the curtain rises.

And now let us return to our old friend Patterson, of *Patterson's Roads*, the compiler of the travellers' vade-mecum of those days, and the man who must have known more of the "cities, market towns, Remarkable Villages, Nobility, Gentry, Antiquities, Natural Curiosities, and other remarkable objects throughout the Kingdom," than anyone else in the world.

To those who do not already know Patterson I would advise a pilgrimage to the dirtiest secondhand book-shop available, where, in a box, labelled in large type, "All this lot sixpence each," they will in all probability find a copy of this guide to the "direct and principal cross roads of England and Wales with part of the roads of Scotland," wherein is given, "remodelled, augmented, and improved in a plan both novel, clear, and intelligible," a table of the population, heights of mountains, and the times of the arrival and departure of the mails from every town in England, together with all the toll-gates at which we must pay, the bridges which we shall cross, and the inns at which we can procure the necessary post-horses.

As the conjurer will tell you when he shows you how his trick is done: "It's so simple."

Once this invaluable work is in our hands, travelling by coach or post-chaise in eighteen hundred and twenty-eight becomes a matter of simplicity itself.

Another great advantage about Patterson is that he is always chatty on a journey. Let us say, for instance, that we propose (with Patterson) to travel from London to Land's End. On climbing into our seat on the top of the coach at the Gloucester Coffee Tavern in Piccadilly, we at once open his invaluable work at page 85, and for every mile of the way from London to Land's End we shall have in front of us the information as we drive down the road, as to whom of the "nobility and gentry" lived in the various seats on either side of the highway, information as to the monuments, obelisks (great pets of our forefathers), and other "natural curiosities" which we shall pass, and the names of the inns and industries, etc., of the country towns we shall drive through; all this local information and gossip being vouchsafed us in a volume which consisted of some 713 pages (octavo) and maps, and which in my case cost the large sum of sixpence: a chatty little person was Patterson.

Having procured this first inducement to travel, we will now set out; but before we do so let us glance at the map of London which accompanies my story.

The showman will now indicate with his drumstick various points in this map, which, although it is only a plagiarism of, and compiled from, other, older, and dirtier maps, is here included as a diagrammatic picture to illustrate the roads, and various ways, by which we left London if we travelled at night by the mail, instead of by the ordinary, slower, and less punctual day stage-coaches.

I make no apology for this plagiarism of maps and other "exhibits," as they say in the police courts. I know from experience something about plagiarism; I am used to it. After all, my puppets are only puppets, copied originally from real life, but now culled from many dusty nooks and corners.

For all that, my cast is to me a real cast, even to the little mail-coaches you see upon the map starting out on their nightly journeys along the tentacles of the octopus of roads I call England.

In these pages we might travel by His Majesty's mail, stage-coach, our own private travelling chariot and four, or the hired post-chaise. Or we might be among the humble travellers who journeyed down the road in the four-mile-an-hour, broad-wheeled, covered wagon, drawn by six or eight heavy horses, which lumbered its way across the countryside like a huge snail.

Before we ring up the curtain, however, let us take a cursory glance at England and the chief historical events and happenings of that time, some of which were connected with the road.

First and foremost,

GOD SAVE THE KING.

In 1828 George IV had been crowned seven years, and the future Queen Victoria was nine years of age. Mr. Canning, the Premier, had died that year, and the Duke of Wellington had been made Prime Minister. The Bubble companies panic of 1825-26 was over, and the battle of Navarino had been won the year before, but no railway had yet been opened; the mails being first conveyed by rail ten years later.

For getting out of London upon the south side we had Old London Bridge still standing, the houses upon it having been removed many years before; and now the new bridge, opened in 1831, was being actively discussed. Southwark Bridge had been built the year Queen Victoria was born, and Vauxhall Bridge three years earlier; besides these, we had Westminster, Waterloo, Old Blackfriars, Battersea, and Putney Bridges, the last two being wooden ones, also Hammersmith old suspension bridge, but not the present one.

The Post Office was then in Lombard Street, that street with a very bad reputation in earlier reigns, but the new Post Office of St. Martin's-le-Grand was in the course of construction. The mails had been carried by coaches as far back as 1784, when, at the instigation of John Palmer, of Bath, mail-coaches first took the place of the riding post-boys as carriers of His Majesty's mails. Twenty-seven mail-coaches now started at eight o'clock nightly from London, conveying the mails to every part of the United Kingdom, while those from the country arrived at the Post Office between six and seven in the morning.

Every main road had its toll-gates for the maintenance and upkeep of the road, although twenty-seven toll-gates near London had been removed by Act of Parliament the previous year.

ISLINGTON TURNPIKE.

Of the roads themselves. In 1818 Loudon Macadam had introduced his method of road-making, consisting of stones broken to six ounces weight, and the use of clean flints and granite chippings, and his son was now Surveyor-General of metropolitan roads.

Before Telford and Macadam, both pioneers of road engineering, took over the mail and turnpike roads, travelling by wheeled traffic was a very serious and uncomfortable proceeding. You might be stuck in a bog at Kensington for a night, or left in the mire of the Dover road, near Dartford, until a farmer and his team could be found to pull you out.

When, however, Telford, by building a sound surface on the Bristol road in 1784, made it possible for coaches to take the place of mounted post-boys for carrying the mails, the main roads began to improve; and in the golden age of coaching, 1828, after Macadam had also introduced his system of road-making, the coach roads were very good travelling.

These roads—mail roads—the Holyhead, Great North Road, Bath, Portsmouth, etc., were not narrow as they are to-day, the York road being often wide enough for six coaches to pass abreast, and in many places thirty yards across. This is amply verified by many coaching prints of the period. Later, when railways superseded most of the road traffic, and the toll-gates, where the toll for the upkeep of the highway was levied, had been done away with, the sides of the roads were often allowed to become grass-grown, owing to the cost of maintenance falling upon the local authority or the old highway boards. Hence the gradual narrowing and encroachment of grass borders which we now see on the once broad mail-coach roads of 1828.

All of which may be perhaps in itself rather heavy going, but if, when you start with me down the roads, both of us have a picture of them clearly visualized in our minds, it will save many explanations during the journey.

A Coach Office.

In 1828, instead of railway stations, we had coach offices and inns, the headquarters of the various large and prosperous coaching establishments.

These inns, from which many of the mails set out, were mostly situated in the heart of the City of London, "The Bull and Mouth" in Aldersgate Street, "The Swan with Two Necks" in Lad Lane, "The Saracen's Head," Skinner Street, "The Spread Eagle," Gracechurch Street, and, coming a little farther west, "The Belle Sauvage," Ludgate Hill, "The White Horse" in Fetter Lane, and "The Golden Cross" at Charing Cross being the most important of them.

William Chaplin, the founder of Chaplin and Co., the well-known carrying firm of to-day, owned "The Swan with Two Necks" and "The Spread Eagle" inns, and himself horsed some 350 miles on fourteen mails that left London nightly, amongst them the Holyhead, Halifax, Liverpool, Manchester, Bristol, Norwich, and many others. To do this he had over 1,000 horses daily at work on the roads.

Another City house on my map, "The Bull and Mouth," was owned by Edward Sherman, who had at this time been its landlord for five years. He horsed the Edinburgh, Glasgow, Leeds, Exeter, and other mails, but as he married three *wealthy* old maids in succession he must have been more of a *business* than a horsey man. Unlike Chaplin, he was never known to have driven a team himself.

Sherman's coaches, with the exception, of course, of the mails, which were made to Government pattern, were all painted yellow on the under-carriage and panels, and were of what was then a very old-fashioned pattern. The stabling at all these big City inns was almost invariably underground.

"The Swan with Two Necks" and "The Bull and Mouth" were the most important and largest coaching inns in the city, taking the place of our Euston and King's Cross railway stations.

THE DEVONPORT MAIL.
The "Quicksilver."

"The White Horse," Fetter Lane, stabled the Portsmouth and Yarmouth mails and many fast stage-coaches, while the Gloucester coffee-house, standing in Piccadilly, where the Berkeley Hotel now stands, and "The White Horse Cellars" near by, were the head offices and starting-points for the West Country mails.

THE SWAN WITH TWO NECKS

The sacks containing the mail were brought down to Piccadilly each evening at eight o'clock from the Post Office in a small, red, two-wheeled mail-cart, drawn by a fast-trotting cob and accompanied by the guard. James Pollard shows these carts in many of his prints of the time.

THE TWO-WHEELED MAIL-CART.

Immediately on arriving at his waiting coach, the guard would put his mail-bags in the hind boot, the slamming of the lid of which was the signal for the coachman to start away on his all-night journey. His Majesty's mails waited for no man.

London streets were mostly of stone, including Piccadilly and the west end of London. Highgate, Kilburn, Paddington Green, Kensington, Chelsea, Wandsworth, New Cross, Greenwich, Stepney, Wanstead, Walthamstow, Hackney and Islington were villages; and Fitzroy Farm and Chalk Farm were farms in reality.

The King had his private road, now the King's Road, Chelsea, from Putney Bridge to the Queen's palace in St. James's Park, and a few "neat houses and gardens" stood between Vauxhall Bridge and Battersea wooden bridge; Tattersall's was behind St. George's Hospital, then the edge of London; Belgravia was not built, although in some places started; Kensington gravel pits and Knightsbridge barracks were outside London. All of which can be so much more easily shown by following the showman with his drumstick as he points across the map than by reams of printed matter.

The mails here depicted started along the actual roads upon which they are drawn, and the accompanying diagram shows where each mail branched for its final destination.

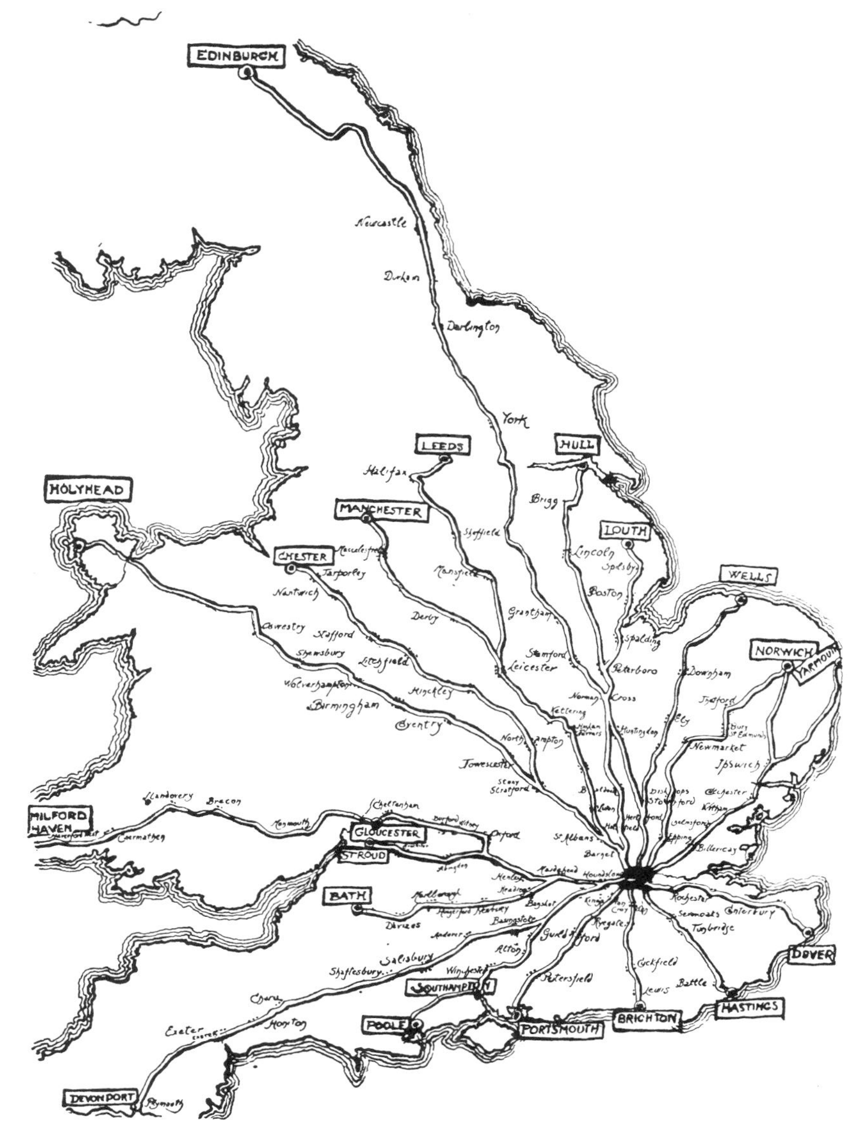

"THE OCTOPUS OF ROADS I CALL ENGLAND."

These were the mail-coach routes, along each of which at eight o'clock nightly my little coaches went galloping across the map of England; and we will now take a glance at the mail itself.

Seven passengers only, three outsides and four insides. The guard, wearing the King's uniform, was a Government official, and not a servant of the proprietors, the people who horsed the mail.

A few of the older coachmen wore the red and gold, and were allowed to do so as a reward for long service, but they were not official

GALLOPING ACROSS THE MAP

servants of the Post Office, their wages being paid by the coach proprietors. The guard had his clock in a sealed case which he carried slung over his shoulder, and was responsible for seeing that the coach ran to its time-table, the reason for the late arrival of the mail at any place having to be clearly stated on the time-sheet or the way-bill which he carried. His clock was set nightly at the Post Office and handed to him in its case as he left the guards' room to pick up his mails.

THE COACHMAN.

So accurately did the mail-coaches run to their time-tables that, in country towns, we could safely set our watches by the time of the arrival or departure of the mail, instead of as we now do by the striking of Big Ben on the wireless.

The mail-coaches themselves were all made to one pattern, and supplied by Messrs. Vidlers, of Millbank, the " proprietors " paying them a rate per mile of running. In reality, these coaches were only carriers of the mail-bags and their guard, the Government servant, on a specified contract with the Post Office; the proprietors or men who horsed the coaches (generally large inn proprietors) taking all the moneys received from carrying the seven passengers allowed by law, and also the small parcel traffic, though this was sometimes a perquisite of the coachmen.

Men like Chaplin or Sherman would undertake a contract with the Post Office to horse and run the Edinburgh or other mail, and would then get other partners or " proprietors " to join in horsing it over the middle ground, etc.

The wording in gold lettering upon these coaches only varied in the name of their destination and the number on the hind boot; but on the stage-coaches the body, and fore and hind boots, were often liberally plastered with the names of the various towns through which the stage passed on its journey; and the colour of the under-carriage and body varied from red, blue, or yellow, whilst on the mail-coaches the coloured portions were always red.

THE GUARD.

Frost or snow, hail and shine, these little coaches went galloping nightly across the map; and when one reads that a celebrated coachman—

Charlie Holmes, to wit—was presented with a piece of plate by admirers and friends after driving the mail 598,000 miles in twenty-six years, it gives some idea of the hardihood of the men of the box seat!

I can hardly see a modern chauffeur driving, at night, 23,000 miles a year with no adequate protection for himself from the vagaries of our English climate. Holmes performed this feat for his employers, Messrs. Costar and Waddell, without having one single accident; the old stage coachmen could certainly teach our chauffeurs of to-day a very great deal.

Such, then, were the coaches in which we rode and undertook our journeys: at that time travelling on the mail costing us about fourpence a mile outside, and fivepence inside, while we paid more if we travelled by post-chaise, and a little less if we travelled by stage-coach.

A Private Travelling Chariot and Four.

If we journeyed in our own private travelling chariot and four, we travelled *de luxe*, but we did *not* have a new carriage every one or two years as we now do: the family coach being handed down as an heirloom from father to son. The more wealthy sent on relays of horses for the shorter journeys, or might hire post-horses where necessary, to draw his lordship and his lady in their own carriage across the country.

Not so many years ago I was met one evening at a station in Rutlandshire by a carriage with a postilion and pair of horses. Although I had only a short distance to travel to my host's hunting-box, the view of the rider bobbing up and down as seen through the front window of this carriage remained for a very long time in my memory.

Through the two little windows in front of the family chariot, or the hired post-chaise—this was the view our forefathers had for hours, and even days at a time, when travelling. Even on my short journey this vista had a distinct monotony after a mile or two; on an all-day journey it must have been very trying to the nerves. Up and down, up and down, up and down, mile after mile, the hind view of a pair of horses and a small man rising and falling in his saddle. The right-hand seat in a post-chaise was certainly the one to scramble for, for there you had only the riderless horse to block the view.

I think that, notwithstanding the possible buffets of the weather, the top of the coach (a real bird's eye-view of the country as compared with the worm's eye-view we get in our "sports model" to-day) must

POSTING.

have been better "going" than the back eye-view of the postilion always in front of us when we travelled by post-chaise.

The post-boy himself was often an interesting character, although his life could not be called one of ease and luxury.

Large posting-houses always had these boys standing about in the

A BIRD'S EYE-VIEW OF THE COUNTRY.

inn yard waiting in sequence for their turn to take the road. The one next on the list to go out was always booted and spurred, with his false leg (which saved his own being damaged by the pole) ready adjusted, and his pair of horses standing on the pillar reins; the then well-known call up the yard, "Next pair out," being his cue to start a stage in either direction, at any time of the day or night.

A little group of these post-boys, small men of the jockey type, your showman produces for you. You will note the high choker tied post-boy fashion often over the chin, while in rough weather the long drab over-coat, well split up the back, covered the short page-boy coat, leathers, and top-boots. Of these latter coats the colour varied, yellow being generally the colour in which South of England post-boys appeared, while blue, or even red, was worn by those of the North. Sometimes in the yard a smock was worn over this livery.

Post-boys Waiting for the "Next Pair Out."

At busy times every large inn yard had its six, eight, or ten waiting post-boys; and though they have completely disappeared since the advent of railways, they were such a feature of the roads that they are being given a considerable place in my pictures.

In a country town all the "Blue Boar" boys might be in white beaver hats; while old Tom Grumpy, of the "King's Arms," would put all his post-boys in a black beaver to make them distinctive when on the road.

It would be interesting to know how many men to-day could emulate the performance of a North country boy who took a pair of horses from Easing-wold to York five times in one day, making a total distance of 130 miles—let us hope not with the same pair of horses! Another York post-boy rode for a wager 150 miles on five successive days on the London to York road.

Like our modern waiter, they relied for a living more upon tips than upon the wages they received, their employer generally giving them board and lodging instead of wages. Each "boy" had four horses under his charge, and during busy times would often do fifty miles or more a day.

Many of the older boys had been carriers of the mails before the Post Office sent letters by mail coaches; a hireling post-boy's job was obviously their *métier* when the Government had no further use for their services.

If we can believe the numerous pictures that have been painted, and the prints that have since been made, the plums of the profession must have been in the towns and villages a few miles from the Border. Here, at any time of the day, an eloping pair of lovers might be driven into the yard, the "next pair out" being then the wedding carriage.

What romance! what excitement! for that post-boy constantly to take this wedding carriage to Gretna Green with eloping brides and bridegrooms, where the notorious blacksmith—who, by the by, I believe, was not a blacksmith at all—would probably end their romance. A post-boy's life near Gretna Green must have been almost as romantic as that of the verger in a fashionable wedding church to-day.

However, familiarity *may* breed contempt, and even a continuous stream of runaway couples may have damped the postilion's romantic feelings; but the "kick," as the Americans say, was in the tail, for a bridegroom should always be in generous mood, and post-boys no doubt received handsome tipping for that last stage.

* * * * *

And then at the end, and a long, long way behind mails, stage-coaches, travelling chariots, and post-chaises, we come to our old friend, the snail of the King's highway.

Eight hairy-heeled horses drag her laboriously over the hills and dales of England: almost the oldest conveyance of them all; a broad-wheeled wagon which had survived the mud and bogs of pre-Macadam and pre-Telford roads, and which still retained the nine-inch wide wheels which had sloshed, bumped, and slithered through the mire of the previous century.

Such a picturesque vehicle must be produced on my stage in its entirety—piled inside and out with country produce and parcels, and carrying only a few slow-talking, slow-thinking country people, on its long and wearisome journey at four miles an hour.

THE SNAIL OF THE KING'S HIGHWAY.

But besides the width of her wheels, the broad-wheeled slow wagon had some other interesting features all her own.

Firstly, an old horn lanthorn of the very largest size always hung at the prow of our old friend: the light from which, if they ever had to travel at night, could have only just reached the two wheel-horses' heads, the remaining six being in a state of semi or complete darkness.

Then the driver, who was more often than not also the owner, rode beside his team on a sturdy cob, from the back of which he could effectively use his long and supple whip.

Piled on the top of the overhead covering, we had the chickens in coops, eggs in baskets, and other produce of the farm and country; while the harness jangled with brasses and bosses, and the leather on the gaily-edged, flapping tops of the collars waved from side to side with the slow-swinging movements of the team.

The broad-wheeled wagon may not have been a Bentley of the road, but it certainly took a very important place in any road picture of the period.

Those were our conveyances, instead of our railway carriages or Rolls-Fords of to-day; the only other way of getting about the country being on Shanks's mare or across the back of a hack or roadster.

On the roads themselves we met many people and things which are unknown to us as we dash along them to-day; but the chief feature that would strike us, if we journeyed in 1828, would be the small number of cottages and houses on the great main roads, and, for those who come from over the Border, the number of toll-gates at which we would have to pay. "Saxpence" didn't take us far in those times. One has only to glance from side to side of the modern road to realize how few of the houses stood there one hundred years ago; about one in fifty being the average on any portion of the road, which we can safely say has not been much built upon in recent years.

A century ago London practically ended at Islington, Paddington Green, Tyburn, Hyde Park Corner, etc. etc.

Out in the country on the mail and turnpike roads there was, of course, less building going on than nearer London; but Kensington and Knightsbridge to Turnham Green were gradually getting a continuous straggling line of houses on either side. All around and behind were fields and open country, and this applied to all the main roads out of the metropolis.

A Country Turnpike.

Turnpike gates or pikes, as they were colloquially called, were more frequent the nearer one got to the towns; but the ugly rows of bungalow huts, council buildings, and other monstrosities that border our main roads to-day did not then spoil the landscape.

When we start down the roads themselves we shall notice this more particularly, as we see each gate and many of the inns as they stood at that time.

THE SNAIL OF THE KING'S HIGHWAY

The big posting-houses clustered together at more or less regular intervals, at the six- to nine-mile stages, but we also had the smaller inns and ale-houses dotted continuously along the roads, at many of which drovers and their flocks were accommodated for the night. If we meet a herd of cattle to-day it is unexpected, and we generally skid our car into them; but when we remember that all cattle at that time came alive and by road to feed the inhabitants of London, we can understand the numbers of sheep and bullocks, etc., with which the roads of the earlier part of the nineteenth century were littered.

Droves of 600 or 700 cattle often came down the North Road from Scotland to be turned into food for the London populace, and these black-polled cattle were always shod for their long journey, with shoes something like a half horse-shoe, the Scottish drovers carrying the shoeing irons for this purpose.

TRAVELLERS FOR THE CHRISTMAS MARKET.

Droves of turkeys also walked from Norfolk and other counties in order to catch the Christmas markets. I mean the owners wanted them to be in time for Christmastide (I have my doubts about the turkeys themselves). They had their feet dipped in pitch before starting, to enable them to stand the wear and tear of the journey, which from some parts of Norfolk took two months to complete.

These flocks started in October in order to arrive in London for Christmas, and I imagine that turkeys' legs must then have wanted some devilling before coming to table. As far as the turkey himself was concerned, that was all the "Romance of the Road" he got.

Geese came in the same way, but the other poultry travelled *de luxe* in crates, on the top of the roof, or slung underneath the slow wagons; not much romance here either, I am afraid, for those in the lower berth.

And last of all the dogs; and even they were different from the show specimens of to-day, thank goodness.

Partly because your showman has already introduced you to his canine helper, and also because he has a liking for dogs himself, some of his friends of 1828 shall come up on to the platform, for they also should picture in the "Romance of the Road"—

"Mongrel Puppy, Whelp and Hound, and Curs of Low Degree."

A prologue being but a preliminary performance, only a few of the people we might meet can be paraded. And, as I read, the population of England in 1828 was between twelve and thirteen millions, we can only bring into the limelight a few samples.

The gentler sex (not to-day's product) were robed like some of these you now see before you; but in this attire what a serious undertaking it must have been for them to get to the top of a coach!—the slightest sign of an ankle making our great-grandmothers blush for the next five miles of their journey. How they did it, I don't know; and how, when once up on the roof, they ever got down again without showing almost as much leg as our modern womenfolk is another conundrum.

LADIES FROM DEVONSHIRE.

Nowadays, of course, legs are no treat to us. The *roué's* is a lost art: in fact, there are no *roués* to practise it, which one must presume is a good thing. Notwithstanding this, the *roué* wasn't a bad old bird; but your short frocks, my dears, have just shrivelled him up, withered him and given him nothing to discover. "Romance of the Road!!!" There certainly isn't any now; but let us get back to 1828, when we had some *roués*, and here is one of them—Old "Q," the Marquess of Queensberry, who really does look, and I believe was, a very bad old man. I make no apology for introducing him here, for surely it is the place he would most have loved.

OLD "Q."

Ladies of those days were sadly behind the fashions, with the exception of those living in London. There was a strong line of demarcation between country cousins' dresses and those of their more fortunate sisters whose parents had town houses. In town a lady from Devonshire looked a lady from Devonshire, and not as she does to-day—just like a breath from Paris.

Fashions took longer to filter through to the country towns and villages; ladies' fashion papers did not exist, and consequently there were no advertisements or pictures to tell us exactly what woman wore from the buff outwards. In this again our present-day picture papers and advertisements have perhaps given a last extra flip to the Passing of the *Roué*.

LADIES IN TOWN.

It was not so much on the roads that we met our womenfolk, however; travelling had too many hardships then to tempt many of them, at any rate during the winter months. They simpered and sighed, stayed at home, knitted their husbands' socks, and fashioned samplers, just as our young folk of the female sex do to-day.

WHAT ! ? ? ?

There seems to be a query about that last remark, so perhaps, as he seems to be getting rather out of his depth, it will be safest for your showman to introduce you to some of his male performers.

Now, although from Oxford one sometimes hears rumours to the contrary, our male is no doubt a very smart fellow, and by smart I mean sartorially smart; but as competition is always good for any art, your producer will allow one of his 1828 actors to appear with a contemporary of our own times.

Both are people who helped in the "Romance of the Road," but at different periods.

They shall be introduced to you in the manner in which the cinema captions have it.

A DANDY OF 1928 AND HIS CONFRÈRE OF 1828.

From these two exhibits it will at once be seen how comical was the appearance of our forefathers as compared with the smartly dressed man of to-day; and no further comment need be made about it.

The early part of the nineteenth century was the halcyon day of the beaver hat, which now is an almost extinct breed.

A cubist's picture of the road at that time would be a collection of beaver hats, or a cubist impression of beaver hats—a feature so eminently suited to his art—and to us of the twentieth century this quantity of top-hats on the road would be a very arresting fact.

Squire, farmer, stage-coachman, innkeeper, traveller, labourer, gamekeeper, tinker, tailor, butcher, baker and candlestick-maker—they all wore the beaver hat.

They wore it in love and in sport, in travel, and of course to church. They went shooting in it, they hunted in it, and fished and played cricket in it; and the only time they discarded it was when they went to bed—when they always put on a nightcap in case their heads should miss it.

Yes, the early part of the nineteenth century was the age of the beaver hat, but even this hat had its waves of fashion in regard to brims, curves, and the height of its crown. Once Sherman, the big coach proprietor of the "Bull and Mouth," almost turned down a celebrated coachman who applied to him for a job because his beaver did not appear to him to have the horsey flatness of brim necessary at that time for the profession of the driver of the mail.

The beaver, the side whiskers, the dark blue spotted stocks, high collars to the coats, brass buttons, innumerable capes to our overcoats, and tight unmentionables (as our forefathers called their trousers) with straps under the instep to hold them in place, were the chief features of their dress in 1828; added to which, when they travelled, they often put on high, untanned gaiters reaching well up the thigh, or wore, if they were obviously "from the country," leathers and top-boots.

Wearers of the Beaver Hat.

But once again let me parade a few of my male actors of the road in order that you may inspect them before we start our first night journey in the Bath Road mail.

Tinker, tailor, soldier, sailor, apothecary, ploughboy, thief; and here let me mention that when you and I, farther on in my story, take the road together we shall appear on the coaches in appropriate attire.

If you want to have an amusing time without being conspicuous, when in Rome you do as Rome does. When we go to Paris we do not—at least I *hope* we do not—sit in the stalls of the Comédie Française in plus-fours and sports coats; therefore, as we are going down the road in 1828, we will

don the clothes and manners of that period, and so make ourselves inconspicuous travellers.

We have now seen a few of the people, some inns and many of the conveyances, and last but not least the dogs; but the hawkers, peep-show man, the chair-mender, the old sailor, the earth-stopper, and the butcher's boy (whose prototype you may see on his shaggy Exmoor pony in many a Devonshire village to-day), ought all to be brought into the picture, as they were important side-shows of the road of the time.

THE EARTH-STOPPER.

"YOUNG LAMBS TO SELL."

THE BUTCHER'S BOY.

THE CHAIR-MENDER.

THE OLD SAILOR.

THE PEEP-SHOW MAN.

"OLD CLO'ES."

I have called this book *The Romance of the Road*, partly because the road was romantic in those days and partly because, even in these hustling times, every one of us has some romance still left somewhere if we can only get down to it.

Even if you deal in figures all day long, or look at the world through dry-as-dust folios and deeds, the romance is there in your hours of relaxation if it can only be brought to the surface; and it is this that I hope to do by driving with you down some of the mail-coach roads of England one hundred years ago.

Fact can sometimes be romantic, often it is more romantic than fiction. The stacks of material, gleaned from the now unread books and news-sheets of the period that lie before me, prove this in many a page and chapter, but the difficulty of your showman is in the elimination of matter to be included, and not in the quantity available.

To the student this immense crowd of material might have an appeal; page after page of statistics as to coaches, mails, and the road in general might be of interest to the few, but it would be intensely dull to the many. Therefore, the blue pencil has to be ruthlessly used if your peep-show is to be an entertainment and not a dry-as-dust lecture, biography, anthology or index.

That, however, is always the object, and the work, of a producer in any entertainment. If I try to wrap my facts up in the sweetened cake of romance, I hope that they will still remain a story of the road of 1828.

History repeats itself, and to-day we have again the bitter war of the road about to begin.

As steam drove the coaches off the road, so in a few, a very few, more years will mechanical road traction drive steam off the map as far as passenger traffic is concerned.

The same war is starting to-day that began in 1838 when the first mail was sent by rail. As coaching was killed, so will the railways suffer, as soon as every one possesses his own means of road transport and the wealthy and adventurous travel by air. One hundred years hence, no doubt, someone else will be writing a story about the quaintness of travelling by trains and the "incredibly slow travelling" of sixty miles an hour. I wonder?

. . . . FIVE! SIX!! SEVEN!!! EIGHT!!!!

struck the clocks of Piccadilly on Midsummer Eve in eighteen hundred and twenty-eight.

Eight coachmen adjusted themselves on their box seats and gathered up the reins, and eight guards hastily threw the last mail bags into the hind boots of their respective coaches.

BANG! BANG!! BANG!!!

went the eight lids, and the western mails started slowly away from the Gloucester Coffee Tavern in Piccadilly on their nightly journey across England.

"Portsmouth," "Bath," "Exeter," "Southampton," "Gloucester," and "Stroud," followed by "Devonport" and "Poole," moved off in rapid succession; all, with the exception of "Portsmouth," taking the Bath Road as far as Hounslow or Maidenhead, where they spread out in various directions, each mail taking the road which eventually brought her to her final destination.

At the same hour many similar mail-coaches started from the heart of the City of London.

"Edinburgh," "Holyhead," "Chester," "Manchester," and "Leeds" left London on the Barnet Road; "Hull," "Louth," and "Wells" (Norfolk) went through Hertford; "Norwich" and "Yarmouth" travelled together on the Colchester Road; and "Hastings" and "Dover" were companions as far as New Cross pike; the remaining two, "Norwich" (via Newmarket) and "Brighton," making lonely journeys through the night on their respective highways.

Straight into the setting sun, now low on the horizon, the western mails were driven, each boss and terret sparkling as they coyly peeped out from either side of the shadows cast by the leaders' heads.

Coachmen beamed on their passengers, guards waved to acquaintances and friends on the side walk, and even the horses seemed to feel the joy of living and carried themselves with more gaiety than usual.

Click-clock! Click-clock! Click-clock! Clickerty-clockerty! Clickerty-clockerty! rang the sixteen iron-shod hoofs of each team as they struck the granite stones of Piccadilly; while, to the music of the tinkle of the pole chains of the wheelers, the clattering of the bars of

"To the Music of the Tinkle of the Pole Chains."

the leaders, and the hum and whirr-r-r of the four wheels—which gave the bass accompaniment to this nightly orchestration of mail-coaches—the three outside passengers congratulated themselves on the beauty of the evening and the consequent pleasantness of their coming journey.

The "Bath" mail, with its smart home-ground team (three chestnuts and a grey), moved off behind "Portsmouth," and as the horses felt their collars, on the rise towards Hyde Park Corner, one could make the acquaintance of the broad-backed driver of the mail and the narrow-backed passenger who sat beside him. The former takes precedence, for he was the man at the helm.

> O'er all his passengers he reigns as king;
> Yet unto every one is underling.

"Broadback" looked what he was—a coachman, the driver of the mail—and did not at all resemble the dapper driver of the Quicksilver ("Devonport"), who looked a gentleman and was one.

For coachmen of the latter sort, who wanted to do away with bearing-reins and use patent safety brakes instead of skids and breeching, "Broadback" had very little use, for he had been brought up in a school which relied on the wheelers to stop the coach by sitting into the breeching. His was the rubicund mottled face which denoted exposure to the weather at all times of the year, and the sinking sun now facing him brought out the full flavour of its flaming colours of orange and purple. Deep grooves and lines running in every direction over it made it resemble a map of the roads and lanes through which he took his nightly drive. Born and bred a coachman (his father before him had carried His Majesty's mails as a post-boy), he handled his team like an artist as he sat on his raised seat on the off-side of the coach. Quietness was his method of driving four horses, however ill-assorted a team they might be, and even "three blind 'uns and a bolter" had no terrors for him or the passengers who knew him, when once he had adjusted himself on the box seat.

When punishment was needed no driver could administer it more quickly or more accurately than "Broadback." The point of his thong was the quickest thing on the coach, and woe betide the near leader or any other member of the team who was not doing his share of the work. "Quietness and quickness" was his motto, with both his reins and whip. He was never bustled and never in a bad hurry. He learnt his apprenticeship in a hard school when coach horses were not of the quality of the teams he now drove, days before the advent of Telford and Macadam, when roads in winter were often axle-deep in ruts and it took two days to get from Oxford to London.

Then his wretched wheelers learnt to know the rattle of the "Short Tommy" which had to be brought out to "assist" them in dragging

"BROADBACK" AND "NARROWBACK"

their load up steep hills, and with which he or his passenger would belabour them from the box seat.

Bad teams and deep ruts had now completely disappeared on all turnpike roads, and this "Short Tommy" was a thing of the past; but when he first became a driver it had been an unpleasant necessity if he wished to get his coach to the end of the journey.

His white hat had the curl of the Regency bucks instead of the smart coachman's beaver of '28 which had a brim as flat as a pancake. His many chins were wrapped round with a blue bird's-eye-spotted scarf, which was tucked into one of the great-coats which he always carried; the rest of this coat collection, in various degrees of age, disrespectability and suitability for all kinds of climatic conditions, being safely and warmly tucked away beneath his huge body, their numerous capes often protruding like a hammer cloth over the back of his box seat.

Under the light overcoat which he wore thrown open was seen the red and gold of His Majesty's livery, the wearing of which, by the coachman—as we already know—plainly denoted that he had been many years on the mail service, and was a trusted servant of both "proprietors" and the Post Office. He was almost the only driver of the procession who wore this livery, of which fact he was very proud.

Long tan gaiters reached half-way up his thighs, almost covering the strong cord breeches in which they were encased, while his boots were of the description which denoted a leaning more to comfort than to elegance.

Notwithstanding his knowledge of the inns on the road, he had a great contempt for what he called "the new beer shops" which were then springing up on all the turnpike routes. The old inn with its archway entrance for his coach, and its snug bar parlour and coffee-room for himself and his passengers, was what he most admired—an inn where you could stay the night should you wish to do so, and where the buxom landlady would herself see that all your wants were attended to.

He knew the exact stone at which his coach should stop when he came to the change, and roundly cursed the ostlers if the fresh team were not waiting for him each night at this very spot. Leaders had to be ready coupled together, wheelers fifteen feet behind them, with

"THE OLD INN HE MOST ADMIRED."

one horse on each side of the road, as, like a ship gliding up to the quayside, he brought the body of his coach to a standstill between them. But two minutes he allowed for each change, his guard giving a helping hand when he was not otherwise engaged with his Post Office duties.

He was rather fond of talking to his passengers and, although always keeping an eye on his horses, would tell them many stories of the road and give them advice as to the inns which they passed during the night.

On his galloping stages he would generally hum a tune to himself as he watched his team to see that the coach did not start "rocking"—a dangerous proceeding which, unless care was taken to counteract it in its initial stages, might end in disaster.

He could remember the time when the box seat was embedded in the front axle tree and not attached to the body of the coach, and when the less wealthy of his passengers sat in a basket contraption which rested on the back axle tree, only the body of the coach being then hung on springs.

To that celebrated M.F.H., Mr. John Warde of Squerries—who from 1797 to 1808 rode over the Pytchley country as Master—he always gave the salute with his whip, for he it was who persuaded the proprietors and the Post Office to allow the coachman's seat to be attached to the body of the coach instead of to the front axle, an innovation which added so much to the comfort of the drivers. Previous to this alteration the continual jolting and vibration which the coachmen received was supposed to prevent them falling asleep on the journey; and I have no doubt, considering the deep ruts encountered in the early days of coaching, it most certainly must have done so!

It is quite possible that the Brobdingnagian proportions of our friend's figure were caused by so many hours of his life being passed sitting on the box seat of a coach; but no doubt it was helped by what he apparently thought was the dry nature of the English climate, and the frequent libations at his favourite inns which seemed necessary to counteract the effects of this atmospheric phenomenon.

To see him mount to his exalted seat on the box was a lesson in the poetry of motion. He knew to an inch what swing to give to his immense body as he moved each foot from hub to step and step to footboard, and landed himself exactly over the seat prepared for him. When driving his horses his huge back acted as a welcome protection from the wind and weather to the traveller sitting behind him.

It has been said that a back view often shows as much character as the reverse side of the picture.

The narrow back of the passenger who sat beside the driver perhaps gave some key to the occupation of its owner. Not an athlete, and certainly not a D'Orsay or an Adonis, he might have been taken for a distinguished member of the Antiquarian Society, the proprietor of a secondhand bookshop, or the editor of the *New Spectator*.

Old, short, wizened, with rather long, grizzled grey hair, he wore a low-crowned Pickwickian top-hat which, in windy weather, he made more secure upon his head by tying a bandana scarf completely around it. Large horn-rimmed spectacles shaded his rather sunken eyes, but his skin, plentifully covered with wrinkles, had none of the ruddiness produced by being constantly exposed to the elements which characterized the face of his companion on the box seat. Snuff-coloured

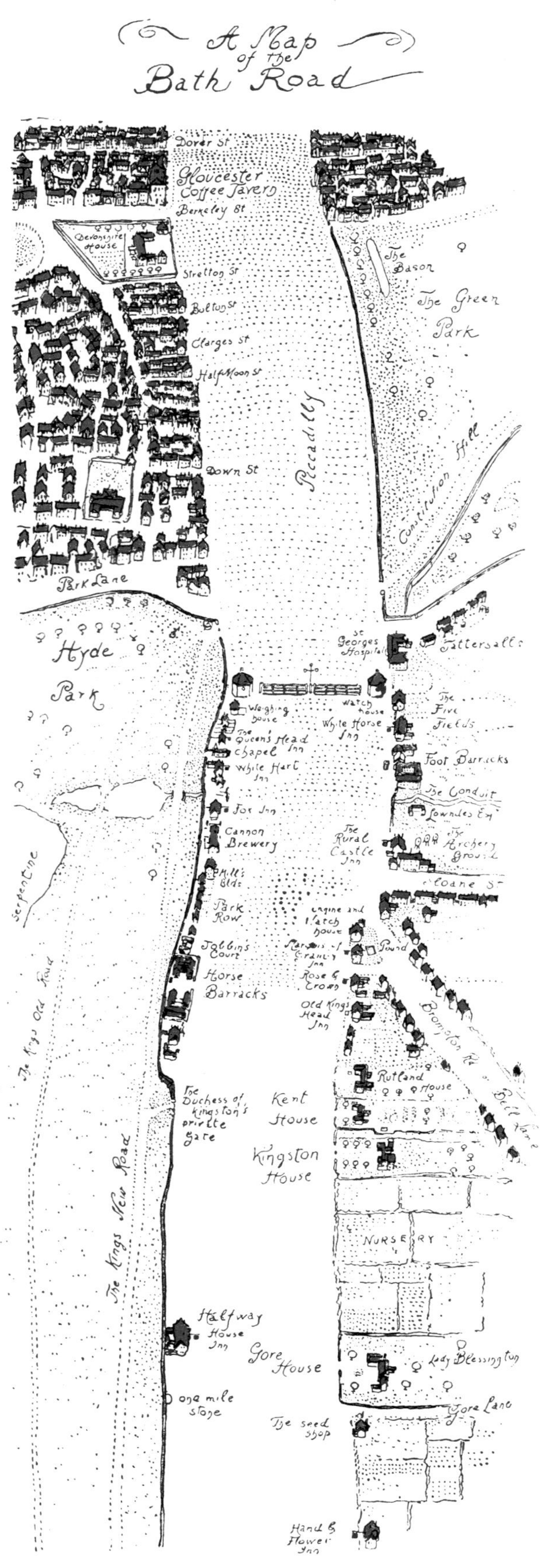

was his coat, snuff-coloured with age was his hat, and snuff-coloured was everything about him, the only exceptions being his red woollen muffler and the voluminous green umbrella, without which he never travelled.

A little vague, a little nervous in his manner, but withal of an inquiring and kindly nature, he had a fund of information upon every topic.

By the time the procession of mails had passed Hyde Park Corner, from which point the milestones of the Bath Road began, a serious start on their journey had been made.

Straddled across the road, about two hundred yards below St. George's Hospital, came the first toll-gate, now thrown wide open to allow "Bath," "Portsmouth," and the mails following to pass through.

Here, on the near-side, was also the first of the watch-houses, which, with their picturesque but useless old watchmen, were to be entirely superseded the following year by the new top-hatted police force.

Then came the White Horse Inn and the Foot Barracks (demolished in 1836 to make way for Belgravia); after them the road crossed the conduit which carried the Westbourne, and then, with but a few small houses in between, came the Rural Castle Inn, near Sloane Street, with an archery ground behind it.

At this time Belgravia was not built, and the end of London was at St. George's Hospital and Apsley House.

The new gates had that year been erected at Hyde Park Corner, and the brick wall from these ran past the toll-gate and behind the houses and the Horse Barracks, when it again appeared at the road-side and continued to Kensington Palace Gates.

From Sloane Street, continuing on the near-side, came the entrance to the Brompton Road or Bell Lane, at which point "Portsmouth" separated from the others to journey over Putney wooden bridge and join the Portsmouth Road on Putney Heath, the other seven guards giving her a few farewell notes on their horns to wish her good night.

At the juncture of Brompton Road with the highway stood Knightsbridge Green, where another watch-house appeared, and also the usual adjunct to village greens, a now disused pound.

Then followed three inns, the "Marquis of Granby," the "Rose and Crown," with its big galleried yard, the "Old King's Head," and a few smaller houses, and after this came open country and large mansions and grounds.

From Hyde Park Corner, on the park side, after the toll-gate was the weighing house, a row of houses, the Queen's Head Inn, Knightsbridge Chapel, and the White Hart Inn. In front of the inns two or three old trees still flourished by the side of the highway; and the chapel, although acknowledged by a contemporary writer to be "a hideous erection," had some interest about it. It was built in 1595, originally as a lazar house, and a railed-off portion of Knightsbridge Green was at one time the burial ground belonging to it.

The driver informed his passengers that this part of the road, from Hyde Park Corner to the "old court suburb" of Kensington, had the distinction of being the first piece of road outside London to be lighted with glazed oil lamps: this was done on account of the numerous footpads who frequented the area, and the consequent danger to the public who journeyed after dark from the Court, when at Kensington, to the town of London.

He could remember the time when a bell was rung at night at both the Kensington and Hyde Park Gate ends in order to collect together foot passengers who, for their own protection, wished to journey in company on this portion of the highway.

Almost opposite Sloane Street was the Cannon Brewery (upon the site on which the Albert Gate now stands), and a little farther on, the Fox Inn, whose sign had been painted by Sir Joshua Reynolds.

The pen-posts of the old cattle market were still dotted along this portion of the route, and a few rows of houses and courts joined up with the present Horse Barracks.

At this point the granite setts ended, and the brick wall of Hyde Park once more lined the highway—one half-mile from Hyde Park Corner.

And now, on the opposite side of the road, Rutland House, Kent House and Kingston House were passed in rapid succession, into the gardens of which the passengers had been able to see owing to their elevated position on the coach top.

Rutland House had Lord Campbell as its tenant, although, as its name suggests, members of the Manners family had at one time lived in it.

In Kent House also once lived the Duke of Kent (the father of Queen Victoria), before he moved into Kensington Palace.

But about Kingston House, both "Broadback" and "Narrow-back" had much to say. Built in 1769 for that sensational Court figure, Elizabeth Chudleigh, it occupied the position upon which once stood Paradise Row.

About the time it was erected, Elizabeth married the Duke of Kingston, although, as it subsequently transpired, she was already the wife of Augustus John Hervey, Earl of Bristol. (Incidentally our coachman mentioned that Richard Tattersall, the founder of Tattersall's Yard, was at that time training-groom to the Duke.)

Elizabeth Chudleigh was descended from an old Devon family, and was the daughter of a Colonel Chudleigh. At the age of eighteen she obtained the post of maid of honour to the Princess of Wales, wife of Frederick, Prince of Wales, and the mother of King George III. Soon after this Elizabeth became engaged to the Duke of Hamilton, who was then about to undertake the grand tour. Whilst he was away, however, Elizabeth met Captain Hervey, a son of the Earl of Bristol, and Hervey fell desperately in love with her. The lady herself does not seem to have returned his passion, although her aunt, whom she was then visiting, did all she could to advance his suit.

It appeared that the aunt even went so far as to intercept the Duke of Hamilton's letters to his fiancée, and Elizabeth, piqued at the Duke's apparent neglect, accepted the pressing suit of Hervey and consented to a secret marriage. This took place in the private chapel of a friend's house on August 4th, 1744.

But Hervey was not so successful as a husband as he had been as a lover, and in a very short time his wife decided to have nothing more to do with him. The secret marriage being still unknown at Court, she was able to retain her position as maid of honour to the Princess of Wales, and, as Hervey was very badly off, the salary she was receiving from this appointment seems to have been a lever for forcing her husband to continue to keep their union secret.

In the meantime the plot thickened, and the Duke of Hamilton, still in love with Elizabeth, returned to England!

At once he pressed his suit on the lady, but, to his astonishment, his advances were now treated with a coldness which he was unable to understand.

In the end, thinking that his fiancée must have changed her mind during his absence abroad, he gave up all further claims to her hand, at a later date marrying one of the three beautiful Miss Gunnings.

Mrs. Chudleigh and her friends, not knowing of Elizabeth's marriage, thought her a fool, and told her so, but no whisper of her secret then transpired, and so for the time being the matter ended.

At last things became so unendurable at home that the lady determined to travel, and reaching Germany was received at the Court of Frederick the Great, where she became extremely popular and stayed for some time.

On her return to England "Miss Chudleigh" (as she was still known to the world) became the toast of the town and cynosure of all eyes. Whether "playing cards at Lord Chesterfield's," "acting at Lady Harrington's," or appearing at one of the masked balls which were then the fashion, her striking beauty and personality always attracted attention.

A portrait of her in the costume (or rather want of it) in which she appeared at one of these balls, as Iphigenia, was at that time published and (so we are informed) had a great vogue with the *beaux* of the town.

But poor Elizabeth had not yet got rid of her objectionable husband. Wherever she went, wherever she might hide herself (which if truth be told she does not seem to have attempted to do), Captain Hervey was always somewhere at hand to throw a shadow over her gay life.

At last, worried to death with this continual skeleton in the cupboard, she decided to tell everything to her mistress, the Princess of Wales. Whether this was done or not does not seem very clear, but certain it is that Elizabeth suffered from no loss of prestige at Court, and as the notorious character of Captain Hervey was a byword at the time I daresay she received a good deal of pity from her august patroness.

At this time, whether it was suggested to her or was evolved from her own fertile brain, the idea occurred to her of getting rid of her husband by destroying the evidence of the marriage in the church register. Having gained access to this, she secretly tore out the leaf, returned to London with it in her possession, and then bade open defiance to her lawful spouse.

At this part of the story, however, Elizabeth's character suffered considerably. Some little time after the leaf had been extracted, Captain Hervey unexpectedly succeeded to the Earldom of Bristol, and the lady, no doubt thinking that she might as well become a countess (having missed becoming a duchess), calmly went down to Winchester and reinserted the leaf in the register, having no doubt previously bribed the clerk and others necessary to enable her to carry out her plan. Poor Elizabeth! Nothing seemed to go right with her, for, almost immediately after she had established her claim to the title of Countess, the Duke of Kingston came into her life, and she wished the register and all connected with it at the bottom of the deep blue sea.

Marriage with the Duke was out of the question, but gossip says that the lady, as she could not marry him, became his "chère amie," and lived with him unblessed by the Church.

In a way, the Duke's intentions were honourable, and after much negotiating with Lord Bristol the latter agreed to waive all claims on Elizabeth and to offer no opposition to his wife's legal union with the Duke.

It is difficult to understand how these three thought the legal and ecclesiastical sides of this union could be established, but there is no doubt that the ceremony of marriage was performed on March 6th, in 1769, between the Duke of Kingston and the Countess of Bristol, her husband, the Earl of Bristol, being very much alive at the time.

For some few years, as Duchess of Kingston, and living at Kingston House, Elizabeth became a leader of fashion, but in 1773 the Duke died and troubles once more began to surround her.

After her so-called husband's death, the Duchess travelled to Italy and was entertained by the Pope and other influential Italians; but while she was abroad a witness to her original marriage with Captain Hervey (as he then was) turned up (exactly as they used to do in the old plays at the Adelphi), and, being in reduced circumstances, applied to the Duchess's solicitor in London for help: in plain words, I expect, threatened blackmail.

This help was refused; and Mrs. Craddock, the witness before mentioned, immediately went to the late Duke's relatives and told them the whole story. Without more ado proceedings were commenced by them against the absent Duchess, and Elizabeth, on hearing this unpleasant news, at once hurried home.

On April 15th, 1776, the trial of the widowed Duchess of Kingston, "for the crime of bigamously marrying Evelyn Pierrepont, Duke of Kingston, her first husband, Captain Hervey, afterwards Earl of Bristol, being then alive," was commenced and continued for seven days. Elizabeth was found guilty, but, pleading the privilege of the peerage, was discharged; instead of suffering the punishment for bigamy, which at that time was transportation or imprisonment.

And now this little matrimonial jack-in-the-box had to put back the clock and become known as the Countess of Bristol; and as very strong efforts were being made, as she no doubt expected they would be, to deprive her of all that the Duke of Kingston had left her in his will, she was advised to leave the country.

But Elizabeth, having gone through life so far making dramatic situations, could not make her last exit from English soil without some striking pose.

In order to put the world off the scent, and wishing to leave England secretly, she ordered her carriage, on the day of her departure, to be driven through the fashionable parts of London as if flight was the last thing she contemplated. Also, to make secrecy more secure, she invited a large party of friends to dine at Kingston House on that day, who upon their arrival found an empty house and their hostess flown.

First at Calais, like so many of England's defaulting creditors, and afterwards near Paris, Elizabeth took up her abode; at the latter place installing herself in an immense house which, we regret having to state, was the property of the French King's brother.

Then comes her final dramatic end. After her flight, a lawsuit had been pending about another estate which she had purchased, no doubt with some of the Duke's money, and, on hearing that the verdict had been given against her, the lady flew into so violent a temper that she burst a blood-vessel and died from the result of it on August 26th, 1796.

The story of her life was published at the time in two pamphlets entitled "An Authentic Detail of Particulars Relative to the late Duchess of Kingston" and "Original Anecdotes of the late Duke of Kingston and Miss Chudleigh," published by Thomas Whitehead, in the year 1792.

Elizabeth Chudleigh! Countess of Bristol!! Duchess of Kingston!!!—we take off our hats to you—why, oh why has your story never been given to us in play or picture? Truth is stranger than fiction. No novelist or producer ever thought out a better plot, and no playwright or actor ever had a more romantic character to depict.

On the opposite side of the road to Kingston House, and in the wall of the Park, stood a padlocked gateway which "Broadback" stated had always been known as the "Duchess of Kingston's Gate," and which, he understood, was a private gateway granted to the lady by permission of the Regent when Prince of Wales; but the passenger beside him affirmed that it was much more probable that the gate, and permission to use it, was granted by the former Prince of Wales, Frederick Lewis (son of George II, who died in 1772, the year before the Duke of Kingston), to whose wife Elizabeth was a maid of honour for so many years.

Be that as it may, the gate was there—the house was there—and the Duchess of Kingston was certainly for a short period there; but in the year of which I am writing the owner was the Earl of Listowel, who purchased it when he was Viscount Ennismore.

And then on this park side of the road, all alone with its sinister reputation, stood the Halfway House Inn.

Here we had a remnant of past days, of the mud, mire, and highwaymen of this part of the road, a house that once was the gazebo and meeting house of "gentlemen of the road."

It was here that the highwaymen's touts forgathered, ready to send word to Hounslow Heath and other notorious places on the

"All Alone with its Sinister Reputation."

western roads when wealthy families or merchants were starting on a journey; and here it was that the father of our coachman, when a post-boy in 1740, was robbed by highwaymen, his assailants getting away with both his horse and the Bath and Bristol mail-bags.

From Kent House one came to Kensington Gore, "the second from the left, with white stucco over the front," being the house once occupied by John Wilkes. He was the London alderman, and M.P. for Aylesbury, who in 1763 was arrested and committed to the Tower for libelling the King, while his paper, the *North Briton*, was publicly burnt by the hangman. The reason for this was that he had charged the King with uttering "inexactitudes" in his speech. Wilkes was arrested on a "general warrant"—a warrant which did not specify the name of the accused, and which was subsequently declared

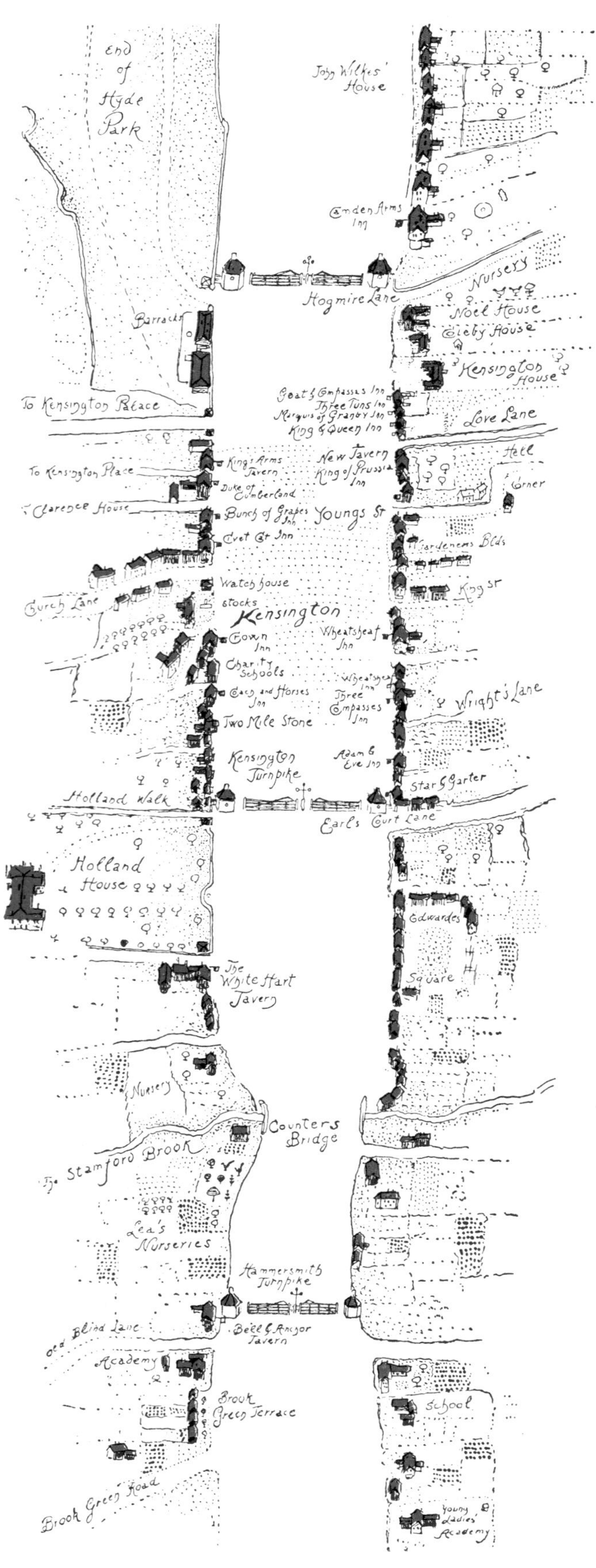

by Parliament to be illegal. On December 6th, 1763, he received £5,000 damages, and was made Lord Mayor of London in 1774. The following year an obelisk was erected to him in Fleet Street, at the top of Bridge Street; a man of many vicissitudes, both amorous and financial, he died a bankrupt in 1797. We have often had his prototype in our own times.

Gore House was opposite the first milestone from Hyde Park Corner, and stood upon the site upon which the Albert Hall now stands. It had had a variety of tenants—owners both grave and gay, for in succession it had housed a miserly financier, a great philanthropist, and a talented, but I fear—God bless her!—a somewhat frail beauty.

Of the first, named Morgan, it was said that with an income of £10,000 a year he never spent one penny on the house, and when the good William Wilberforce, of Abolition-of-Slave-Trade renown, succeeded him in 1808, the property was in a very bad state of repair. Here Wilberforce lived until 1823, when the beautiful Lady Blessington, who was then a widow, became the subsequent tenant. With her at that time

THROUGH THE OPEN TOLL-GATE

lived Count D'Orsay, one of my puppets who has already appeared in picture on page 22 of my story, and here for some time forgathered many of the most brilliant men of the period. In 1849 the usual *débâcle* of the owners of houses of this part of the Bath Road took place, for in April of that year Count D'Orsay and Lady Blessington were besieged by creditors in Gore House, and a sheriff's officer put in an execution and took up his unwelcome abode with them.

D'Orsay fled to France, the lady quickly following him, but she died of heart disease one short month after her arrival on French soil.

The Duchess of Kingston (or Countess of Bristol), Lady Blessington, and John Wilkes all seemed to have met the same financial fate within a few years, and all lived in houses almost touching each other.

It was just about here, too, that some two years earlier the Reading coach had been overturned on its way to the Bolt-in-Tun Inn, Fleet Street. The *Times* of March 7th, 1826, commenting on the accident which had been caused by a wheel coming off, suggested that "Some official ought to be employed to examine the wheels of all public carriages at every stage"; but I don't think this wise advice was ever taken.

At Hogmire Lane (Gloucester Road) the mails passed through the second toll-gate of the Bath Road, and just below it stood the barracks for troops connected with the Kensington Palace Guard.

Then began the cluster of inns and taverns which marked the entrance to Kensington, with Young Street—leading to Hell Corner and Kensington Square—on one side, and Kensington Church, with the stocks still in front of it, on the other. Young Street was named after the builder of Kensington Square, who lived in the time of William and Mary. Kensington House, with its high wall all round it, was, in the time of Charles II, the country house of the notorious Louise de Querouaille, Duchess of Portsmouth, but in 1828 it was occupied by a Mrs. Inchbald. In after years Baron Grant built his enormous house on this site.

At the King's Arms Tavern the granite setts again began and continued through Kensington—a welcome relief after the dust of that portion of the road which ran from the Horse Barracks to Kensington Palace.

The coachman then driving the Bath mail, and he alone of the twenty-seven mail drivers, had permission to use the King's private roads, i.e. the King's private road in Hyde Park and the one from the Queen's palace (Buckingham Palace) to Putney. Although not always availing himself of this permission, he would proudly tell his passengers how and why it had been granted to him.

King George IV, when staying at one of his country palaces, was sometimes provided by the Post Office with a mail coach, and being specially pleased with one of the drivers gave him a pass to enable him to use the Royal private roads at any time.

A record of this may still be found among the Post Office archives.

After Kensington Church the street narrowed considerably, and here, when the eight o'clock mails went through, the traffic became very congested—stage-coaches, post-chaises, horsemen and travelling chariots, as they hastened London-wards in order to get to town before darkness set in, meeting the mail coaches in one continuous stream.

The slow-moving stage-wagons and market carts, as they plodded on their way, also impeded the coaches' "incredibly fast travelling" of ten miles an hour.

The smell of the road and the noise of the rumble of many wheels rolling over the granite stones filled the air in this narrow part of the way at all times of the day, but on a summer's evening when the seven out-going mails met the in-coming traffic Kensington was in truth a busy village.

A story was told in connection with Coleby House, facing Kensington Palace Gates, which had just been passed—a story with a moral like so many stories of that period, showing the futility of thinking too much of this world's goods.

Sir Thomas Coleby, a Commissioner in the Victualling Office, built Coleby House in the year 1720, and died intestate, leaving £200,000 in the Funds.

In the manner of his death, however, we get the moral, for a writer of the time recorded that Sir Thomas, "rising in the middle of the night when he was in a very proper sweat, the effect of medicine which he had taken for that purpose, and walking down stairs to look for the key of the wine cellar which he had inadvertently left on the table in his parlour, being apprehensive that his servants might seize a bottle of port wine," fell dead—and neither his wine nor his money were of any further use to him. The moral of which so obviously is, that it is better for a rich man to allow his servants to drink a bottle of his port wine than to rise in the middle of the night when "in a very proper sweat, the effect of medicine," to prevent the possibility of them doing so.

Sir Thomas Coleby "Rising in the Middle of the Night."

Almost at the end of Kensington, just as one reached Holland Park, stood Kensington Toll Bar, the third gate on the Bath Road, with Earl's Court Lane just beside it.

Edwardes Square, named after the Edwardes family who lived in Holland House in 1767, was in process of being built; then came Earl's Terrace, with lodges at either end, and after that the open country with only a few houses until one reached Counters Bridge (Addison Bridge), which spanned the Stamford Brook on its way to the Thames at Chelsea.

On the other side of the road, after Holland House, was the

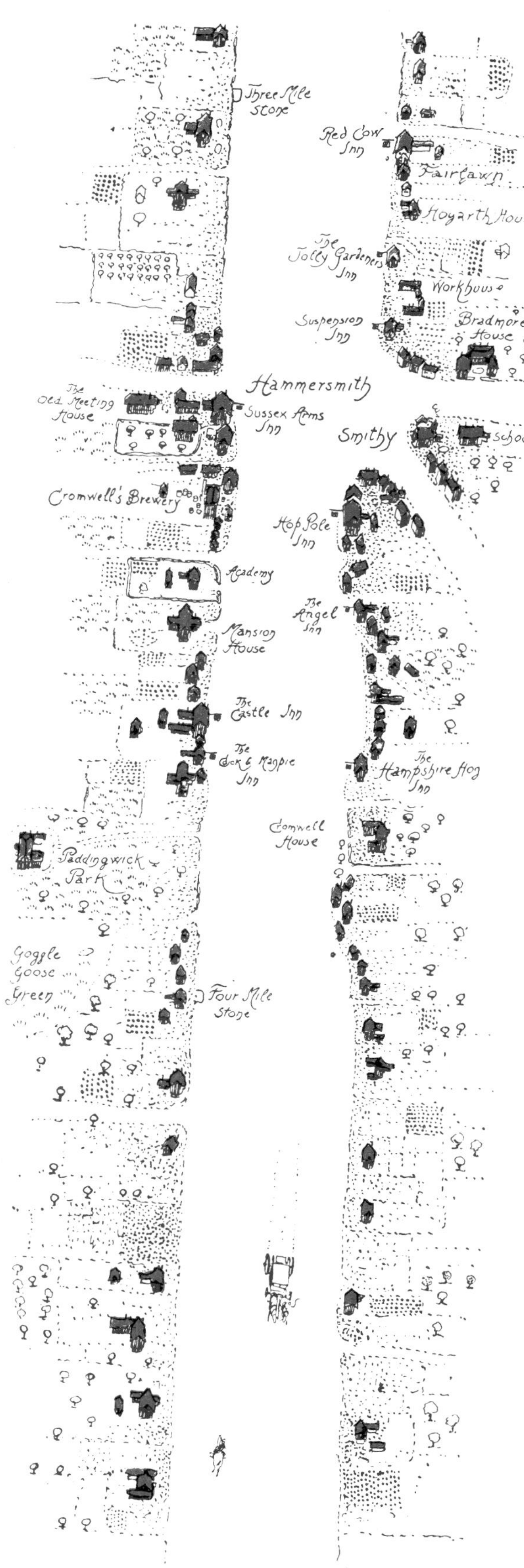

White Hart Tavern, and then again country and nursery gardens as far as Hammersmith turnpike.

Holland House was built by Sir Walter Cope in 1607 and took its name from his son-in-law, Henry Rich, Earl of Holland, who, in 1649, "suffered death upon the scaffold for participating in the last attempt to restore King Charles upon the throne."

Addison became possessed of the house in 1716 when he made his unhappy marriage with the Dowager Countess of Warwick and Holland, and died in it in 1719.

After this the house went to the Edwardes family, who sold it to a Henry Fox who made the wonderful gardens and built a theatre in its grounds.

This owner made a runaway marriage with the Duke of Richmond's eldest daughter, which, unlike most runaway marriages, seems to have turned out to be a lifelong love match. In 1763 he was created Baron Holland, and died at Holland House eleven years later.

It was in these grounds the famous duel between Lord Camelford and Mr. Best was fought, and the former killed.

To the White Hart Tavern, Addison, when in possession of Holland House, would often repair to drown his sorrows, and at the "Adam and Eve" opposite was still preserved a long bill, which he ran up before living at Holland House, which Lord Holland had in the end to pay.

Just over Counters Bridge stood Hammersmith turnpike, and beside it the Bell and Anchor Inn, at which many coaches stopped for their first halt out, or last stop in, when entering or leaving London.

At this house the driver, for the ostensible reason of "delivering a small parcel," pulled in. The rather extraordinary part of this proceeding was that, without any order being given and almost before the wheels of the mail had stopped revolving, a huge tray of flowing bowls appeared, which were immediately handed up to those who required them, to counteract, one presumes, the effect of the dust between Kensington and Hammersmith turnpikes.

In these days of tarmac roads no one except the most confirmed drinker ever gets thirsty on a journey; but what a godsend the dust (then supplied by Mr. Macadam) must have been to the innkeepers on the roads of 1828!

Even on this short journey from Hyde Park Corner to Hammersmith it was agreeable, nay, even a necessity, to have some liquid refreshment in the cool of a summer's evening.

In those days there were certain houses at which the drivers of public conveyances always stopped, and others at which slow wagons, drovers, and flock-masters always pulled in; each type of vehicle and traveller having their own house of call along the route.

"The Bell and Anchor" was one of those houses much patronized by the better class of road conveyance, and it was as much part of the ritual of his nightly drive for "Broadback" to pull up to deliver this fictitious "small parcel" as it was for him to catch up the thong of his whip at starting or to look at the coupling buckles of the reins of each fresh team.

A little farther on, on the near side of the way, stood the picturesque Red Cow Inn, which, at a later date, was a favourite haunt of Charles Keene, the *Punch* artist, and which has many times been made the subject of sketches and pictures. It was here also that a similar robbery of the mail to that of the "Halfway House" took place, but this time the thieves secured the two mail-bags from the post-boy's pony while he was refreshing himself inside the inn.

THE RED COW INN, HAMMERSMITH.

Next door to this inn stood "Fairlawn," the house of Dr. Burney, which in 1828 was an important house on the Bath Road and at that time a school. Dr. Burney was a great classical scholar, and on his death in 1817 his library was purchased by the nation and is now housed in the British Museum.

So far, I am afraid the saying, "His Majesty's mail waits for no man," is being very badly exemplified by what must seem our rather slow progress, and we must pass on through this land of inns, schools, and academies, leaving on our left the road to the new suspension bridge at Hammersmith Broadway, where the forge and smithy stood, and travel on, only noticing a passage-way which runs up between the George Inn and the "Sussex Arms," to which our driver with a knowing wink has drawn attention.

Up this passage, near the old Meeting House at Hammersmith, was a rather large house, surrounded, like the Duchess of Portsmouth's house, by a very high wall—but perhaps, as coachmen's gossip is rather nearly akin to backstairs gossip, the story should not be told . . . . even Royal families are but human beings, and it was rumoured—with how much truth I am not prepared to say—that certain charming

ladies living in this secluded spot were occasionally visited by a Royal personage in a somewhat private-individual way.

For some reason never yet explained, a coachman's ruddy face seems able to put more expression into a wink than anyone else's, so perhaps the rest of this story had best be left to the imagination of my readers. One hopes, however, that this one little scandal of Hammersmith Broadway was not allowed to leak out among the surrounding academies and young ladies' seminaries which housed and educated the prim little misses of that period.

Cromwell's Brewery, in Hammersmith's narrow street, was of course pointed out as a very important local industry; and later on, on the near side of the road, also Cromwell House, which was the home of *James* and not *Oliver* Cromwell; James being the founder of the above-mentioned business. He it was, so "Broadback" told, who started life by himself taking round on a barrow the beer which he had brewed, but who died worth a very large sum of money.

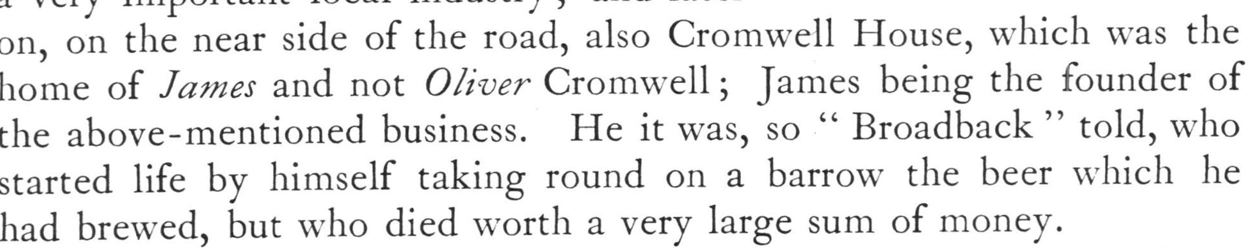

His death took place at the good old age of seventy-five, and was caused by being "overtaken by a seizure" while riding his old horse home from Mark Lane in the City of London.

Near Cromwell House is Paddenswyck, or, as Roque's map (1741) has it, Paddingwick Park, but which we know as Ravenscourt Park. It was then a very old house which had once had a moat surrounding it. Behind the house was Starch Green, where the gibbets stood, and where in 1828 the inhabitants bred rabbits, out of which they seemed to make a considerable income by selling them to the London markets.

On the west side of Paddenswyck or Paddingwick was a village which, if only on account of its name of Goggle Goose Green, should be recorded. Goggle Goose Green! What a fairy-tale rhythm it has, and how it will please our grandchildren! Fancy telling the story of the "Witch of Goggle—Goose—Green" to the Christmas group

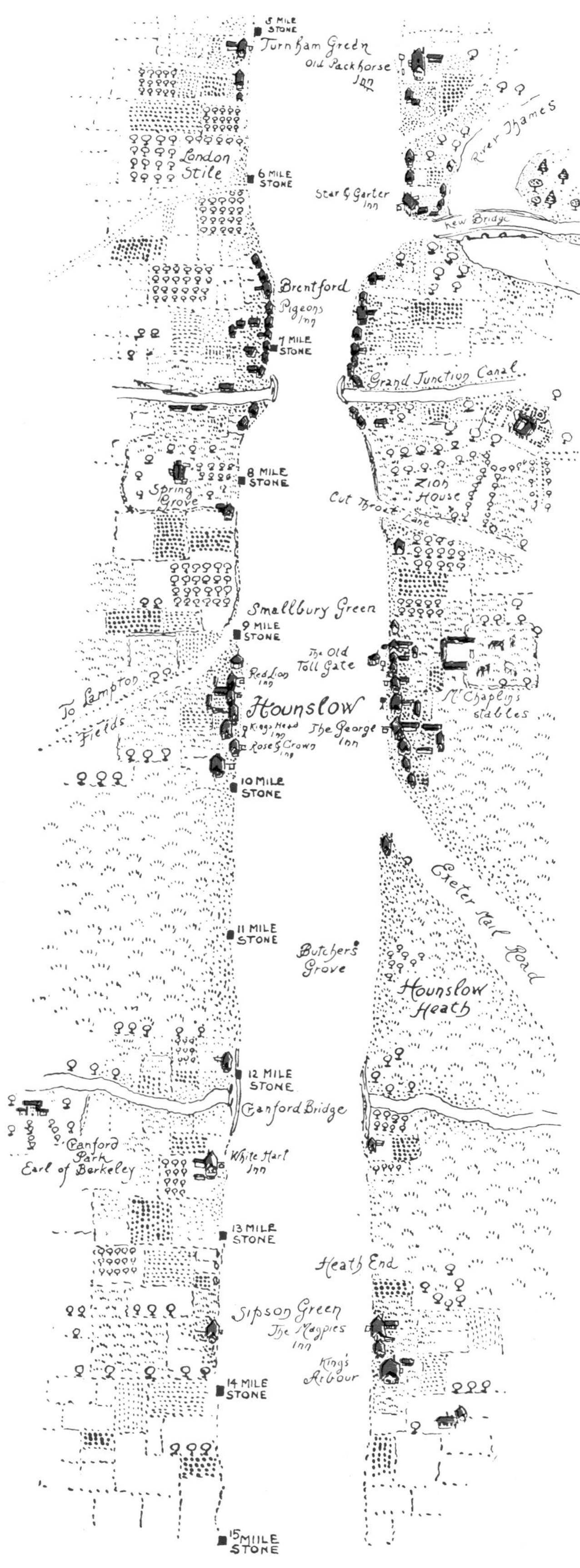

of grandchildren round your ancestral fireside! Think of the widely opening eyes of expectation and excitement as you roll out the name of Goggle—Goose—Green!

The story shall some day be told. It might be squeezed into this volume as a "Romance of the Road," but it would be a little out of place to tell to "Broadback" and "Narrowback" even in the dusk of the evening; so for that reason its telling must be postponed.

Near this Green, on the opposite side of the way, is the avenue of elms leading to the gates of Chiswick House, the seat of the Duke of Devonshire. Sir Walter Scott, when visiting here in the year of our story, was "mightily amazed" at the wild animals kept in the park: the kangaroos, elks, emus, and the Indian cattle cows that were browsing on the lawn, to say nothing of the African elephant which was led about the grounds by an attendant.

At the farther end of Turnham Green stood the "Old Pack Horse," where Horace Walpole always baited when riding from Strawberry Hill to London; and almost opposite this we passed the juncture of the old western road to London through Tyburn

Gate, which at this point joined issue with the one upon which the coaches then travelled.

Once free from the traffic of Kensington and Hammersmith and the fascinating purlieus of Paddingwick Park and Goggle Goose Green (dear old Goggle Goose Green, I hate to leave you), we journeyed more rapidly down the road to Bath.

From here onwards our accompanying maps shall be drawn to ten miles to the page instead of the one-and-a-half miles scale which we have been forced to do if we wished to include all the places and inns we passed when getting out of London.

London Stile, a well-known coaching landmark of 1828, was where the new arterial Great West Road now leaves the old Bath Road, and just past it was the Star and Garter Inn at Kew Bridge.

After passing the turning for Kew and Richmond, we entered the narrow cobbled street of the village of Brentford, which once more relieved the mail passengers from the unwelcome accompaniment

An Inn Yard, Hounslow.

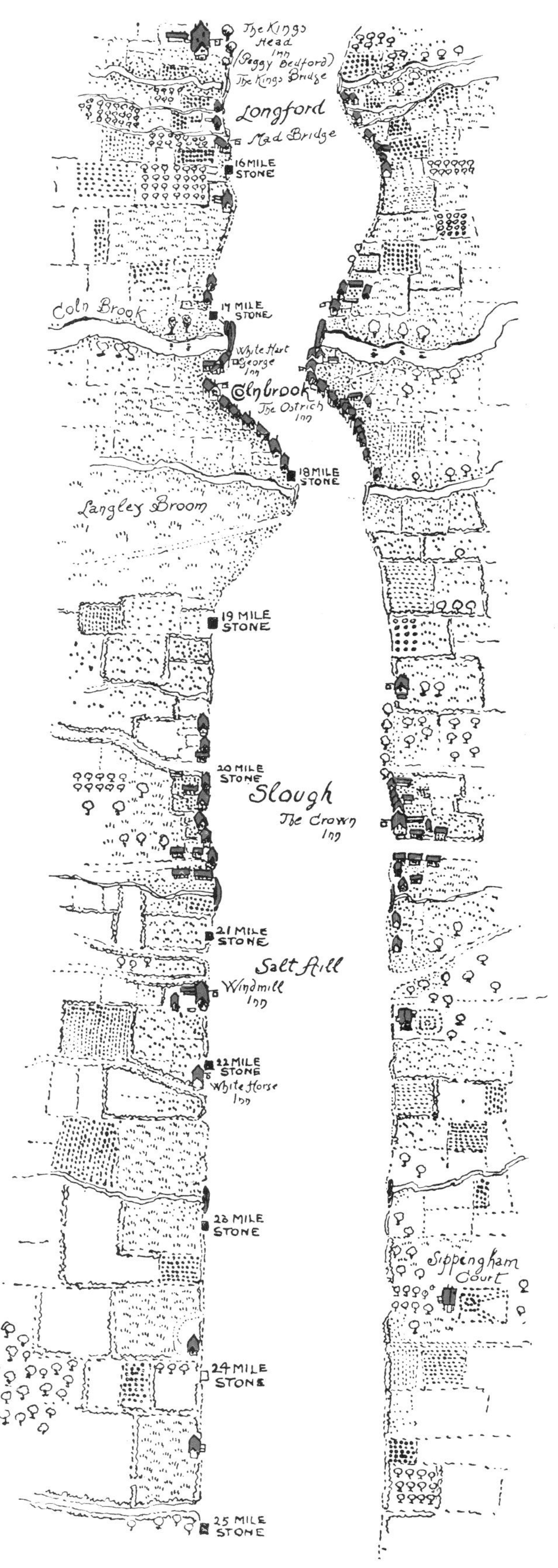

of dust, which began again as soon as the mails passed over the Grand Junction Canal.

Syon House, belonging to the Duke of Northumberland, and Osterley Park, the summer home of the Earl of Jersey, were left behind, and the mail arrived at Mr. Chaplin's stables at Hounslow, where 100 horses were kept, and where the first change took place.

Here, at Hounslow, three of our attendant coaches left the Bath Road; "Southampton," "Poole," and "Devonport" wishing "Bath" good night as they passed, while "Stroud," "Gloucester" and ourselves took the half-right turn across the heath to "The Magpies," King's Arbour and Colnbrook.

Hounslow, a long, straggling, uninteresting village, was chiefly supported by the road; a village of inns and posting-houses and capable of stabling many thousand coach- and post-horses. At this time one hundred and seventy coaches passed through Hounslow daily.

As far back as 1650 it was noted for the number of its inns and ale-houses, but in 1828 the George Inn was the largest and most important posting-house.

Leaving Hounslow, past Butcher's Grove, the mail had Hounslow Heath, with its unpleasant reputation for highwaymen, on the left, with hardly a house or habitation until Sipson Green was reached.

Over Cranford Bridge, past "The Berkeley Arms" and "The King's Arbour"; which latter was a stable used exclusively for His Majesty's post-horses when travelling between Windsor Castle and London.

Peggy Bedford.

At Longford, about one mile from Colnbrook, "Broadback" had apparently another "small parcel to deliver," for the mail was brought to a standstill under the three trees which stood sentinel outside "The King's Head." As at "The Bell and Anchor," at Kensington, so at "The King's Head," this "parcel to deliver" was evidently a nightly affair, for Peggy Bedford, the landlady, was herself awaiting us with another large tray of liquid refreshment in readiness for the passengers on the mail.

And then on past "The Magpies" and over the Coln River the coach travelled, until it arrived at the narrow street of Colnbrook, seven and a-half miles from Hounslow.

A flat and uninteresting stage, but a portion of the road where time could be made up by galloping.

As the team rattled along the old town's narrow streetway, the heavily timbered Ostrich Inn gave welcome from its lighted windows.

This "Ostrich," however, was not always a very hospitable bird. Many years before the house had had a very different reputation, for here many murders were committed, the victims being chiefly wealthy merchants travelling with their merchandise between Bath, Reading, and London.

It is an old story—but because there is a grim humour about it, it shall be told once more.

In the fourteenth century "The Hospice" (now "Ostrich") was very much used by these travellers, and some sixty of them, after staying at the inn, mysteriously disappeared and were never heard of again.

One Thomas Cole (the sixty-first victim) had been for some time ear-marked by the landlord and his amiable spouse for conversion into beer, or, more truthfully, *im*mersion into the brew-house boiling vat, which, by a sinister coincidence, was conveniently placed immediately below the Blue Room bedstead. It was upon this bed (so it was discovered afterwards) that all the sixty victims had slept their last sleep.

"To Empty the Victim into the Vat Below."

Thomas, although he had many times stopped at "The Ostrich," had been difficult to lure into this cosy little room. On one occasion he had brought a friend with him; on another he had been detained at Maidenhead on business about a dog; or had decided that no other than the Pink, Yellow or Green rooms would suit his requirements. It just seemed as if Thomas were to lead a charmed life.

But at last, one night, when he was carrying a considerable amount of specie with him on returning from London to his home at Reading, he was persuaded to use the Blue Room bed.

Now, this Blue Room bed stood on a trap door, which, by releasing a bolt underneath, could be made to empty the victim into the boiling vat below; and our fourteenth-century friend, having in all probability wined himself well before retiring, was duly precipitated into this vat, being found some days afterwards floating in the river.

One or two murders did not much matter in those days, but making a hobby of it—this being the sixty-first—brought the landlord and landlady under the steely glance of the law. Both were arrested, tried, hanged, drawn and quartered, according to tradition, after making a full and complete confession of the whole of the murders.

At Thomas Cole-in-the-Brook the mail changed horses, but *not* at "The Ostrich," whose beer, so "Broadback" asserted, still had a different flavour from that of any other brew in the town.

After passing Colnbrook the continuous stream of market carts with their sleeping drivers, which had been met since Hounslow, almost ceased, and only a few late travellers on the road stirred up the dust on the King's highway, now settling to rest for the night.

The Old Crown Inn at Slough, where Mrs. Catherine Hazell held sway, was the best place to stop in the town, and if we pass it to-day in our car we see it in almost the same state as it was when "Broadback" drove the mail past it, a typical example of the old coaching and posting-house inn.

Catherine Hazell can never welcome us again. No more will the driver of the mail pull up for a "small parcel to deliver"; but the old house still wears its coaching overcoat at any rate, and, as we glide in our mechanical motor on to the cross roads facing it, we feel that we surely are the people who should not be in the foreground of its picture.

Most of the stage-coaches stopped at Salt Hill, just outside the town of Slough, where the Castle and Windmill Inns were the two largest.

The mail changed at the Bear Inn at Maidenhead, at the bottom of the High Street, a house kept by a well-known coach proprietor, W. H. Waddell, whom we have referred to before in our prologue in connection with Charlie Holmes and his testimonial; and at Maidenhead, "Narrowback," like "the man from Cook's," imparted a little guide-book information.

"The Noble Bridge was erected in 1771" (from designs of Sir Robert Taylor) "costing, apart from the land contiguous, £19,000."

It also appeared from records which had apparently been studied that "In the reign of Edward III the town was called Maydenhythe, on account of its large wharf on the river. When the first bridge was thrown across the Thames at this spot in 1297 the name no doubt began to alter, gradually becoming Maidenhead when the hythe itself was done away with."

A list of its inns, which the mail passed by, may not be out of place here, as the names of some of the landlords of that time are familiar to us to-day.

The Inns of Maidenhead in 1828.

"The Orkney Arms," Maidenhead Bridge . . . William Skindle

"The Bear," High Street William H. Waddell

"Red Lion," High Street Richard Lovegrove

"Saracen's Head," High Street Izaac Bailey

"The Sun" (post-horses), High Street . . . . Richard Tagg

"The White Hart," High Street John Russell

THE EVENING STAGE

THE OLD CROWN INN, SLOUGH.

Even in 1792 Archibald Robertson wrote: "At the end of Maidenhead Bridge stands an excellent inn, where travellers are well accommodated and parties often resort together for the amusement of fishing," adding, "and other recreations in the summer months."

Well! well! well! We used to go to dear old "Skindle's" in our callow youth, but I am glad Mr. Robertson in 1792 added that note about "other recreations."

When the mail passed through Maidenhead at 11.25 each night its paved High Street was quiet; but every hour of the day stage-coaches rattled over its stones, and endless streams of post-chaises, horsemen and wagons, on their way to and from Bath, jostled and crowded together in its narrow roadway.

The Bear Inn was the principal inn of coaching times.

At the beginning of Maidenhead Thicket, the "Stroud" and "Gloucester" coaches bade good night to the Bath mail, and took the right-hand road to Henley, but "Broadback's" coach travelled on across the thicket by Little Wick Green to the village of Hare Hatch, by Mr. Girdler's house and Scarlett's, the home of the Lee Parrotts, until Twyford was reached, where at the King's Arms Inn another change of horses was made.

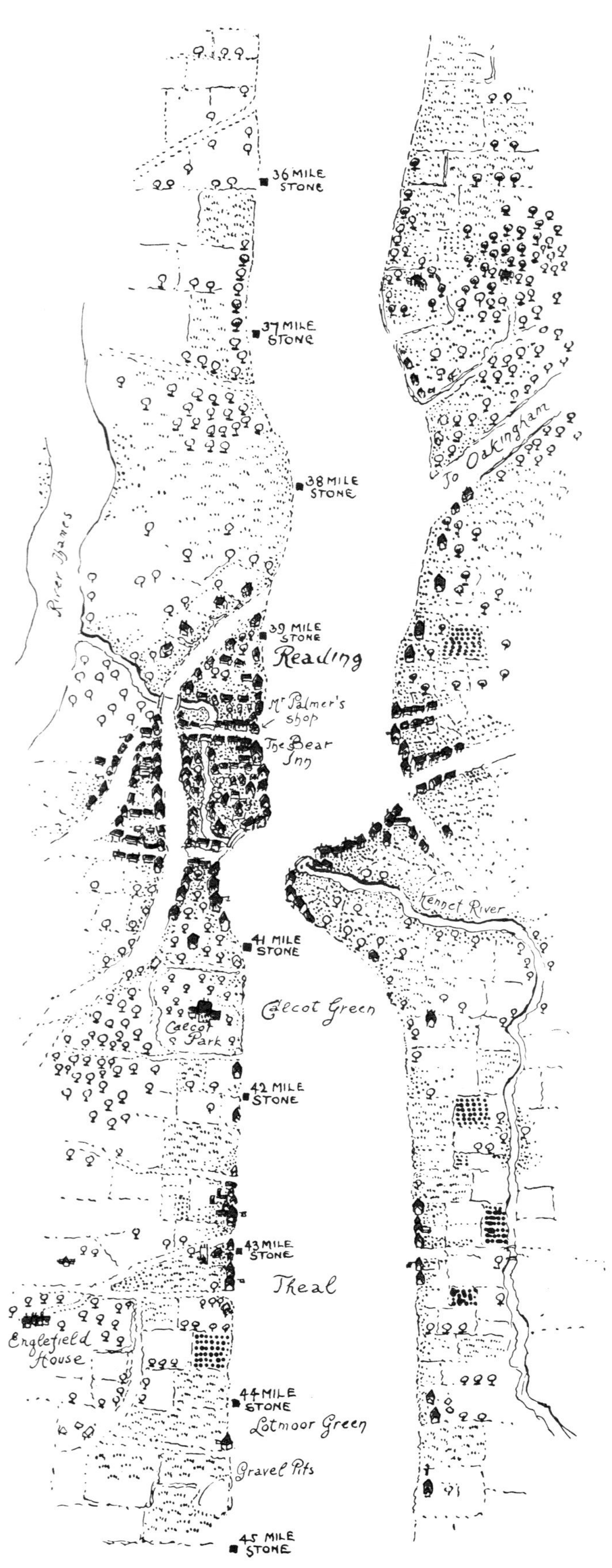

After this she crossed the Lodden River and then along the tree-bordered road which brought her to the top of the hill above Reading, from which in the daytime the first view of the town was obtained.

Rattling down this hill to where the Oakingham Road (now Wokingham) joined the Bath turnpike, she came to the outskirts of the town.

But Reading in those days was not the biscuit town it is to-day, although at the top of London Street, and almost opposite that busy coaching-house, the Bear Inn, stood the original home of Huntley and Palmer's factory, a small and picturesque confectioner's shop.

When the Bath mail passed it, in 1828, at 1.30 a.m., it is possible that its proprietor was asleep in his four-poster, modestly wearing his nightcap.

On the other hand, it is probable that the rattle of the pole-chains of the mail and the notes of the coach-horn may have awakened him from his first beauty sleep.

If this were so, it was more than likely—as a natural train of thought for the keen business mind—that the idea on that

"THE NOTES OF THE COACH-HORN MAY HAVE AWAKENED HIM."

night occurred to him, for the first time, of selling his ginger nuts to the travellers on the Bath coaches the next day, while the horses were being changed at the Bear Inn opposite.

In this way my little Bath mail-coach puppet may have been responsible for the origin of the present great industry of Reading; for certain it is that it was about that time that this idea suggested itself to the proprietor, and that ever afterwards the fame of the ginger nuts made at his little shop spread far and wide among coach travellers.

The subsequent popularity these biscuits acquired, and the money made through selling them, were the foundation stones of this vast business and the stepping-stones to the statue of one of its founders (top-hat, frock-coat, and *umbrella* complete) which to-day greets us as we enter the Broad Street of Reading Town; my only regret is that the original of this work of art should have had so little faith in the climatic conditions of his native town that he would not allow his better half to hold his umbrella for him whilst he posed for the statue.

"To Sell his Ginger Nuts to the Travellers on the Bath Coaches."

Once through Reading, the Bath Road as far as Newbury was fairly level, with only slight galloping undulations, and this part of the road was always kept fairly free from dust by water drawn from the numerous pumps placed at regular intervals along the highway.

These pumps are still standing and line the road as silent sentinels of the coaching era.

Just outside Reading, on the right-hand side of the road, lies Calcot

Park, occupied in 1828 by a Mrs. Boville; but in the early part of the eighteenth century one of its former owners, Miss Frances Kendrick, had given to the world another romance of the Bath Road, the relating of which enlivened the monotony of the night drive towards Newbury.

The lady in question was young, beautiful, and an heiress, but the burly young squires of Berkshire had none of them been able to awaken thoughts of Cupid or Hymen in her apparently cold bosom.

Into Reading one day came Benjamin Child, a young, single, impecunious lawyer, and, as *The Ballad of the Berkshire Lady* tells us, our heroine fell desperately in love with him.

The rest of the story, however, sounds much more modern, and more in keeping with the sort of way our 1928 Miss would handle the matter—for Frances sent Benjamin a challenge to fight a duel with an unknown, not disclosing her identity, and upon the young lawyer arriving at the rendezvous, Calcot Park, he found to his astonishment a masked woman was to be his adversary.

Here was a dilemma for any young and, I can only think, unimpressionable youth—for the story tells us that he had already met Miss Kendrick at some sort of a function, fête, or festivity a day or so before, and that he had not then fallen to her charms, as Frances now fully intended he should do.

"So now take your choice," says she; "either fight or marry me."

A little abrupt, but is what the ballad tells us.

Benjamin, being a lawyer, and no doubt realizing that fighting was against the law, decided very wisely to take the latter course, and the lady then unmasking, he immediately hastened with her, or she with him, I don't know which, to Calcot Church, where the knot was duly tied.

Stout fellow! I agree with Frances that these long engagements are a mistake.

This, however, is only the way I have translated our box seat passenger's story; but anyone who is more interested and wishes for further details can find it all in *The Ballad of the Berkshire Lady,* which was published in Queen Anne's reign about the time of the episode.

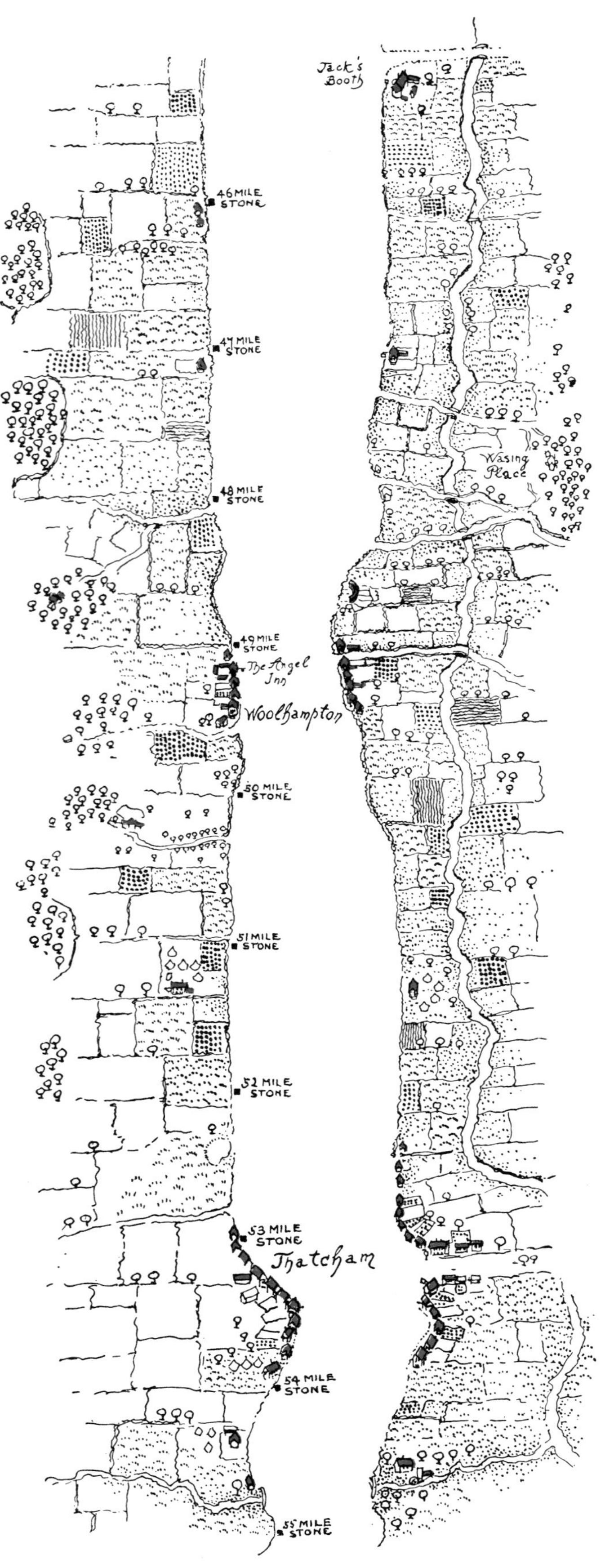

At the Falcon Inn at Theale (or Theal, as we spelt it a hundred years ago) the fifth team for the Bath mail got to work, which took the coach on through Woolhampton to Thatcham, where, at "The King's Head," the next change was made.

And here also it was that "Broadback" left the coach, having driven it 53 miles, and where a fresh coachman was waiting to drive the mail on to Bath. As soon as "Broadback" got down from the box he opened the door to inform the insides of this fact, in case they might wish to "remember" him. "Gentlemen, I leave you here"; which meant the same thing that the wine steward means at a public dinner, when he breathes into your ear as you sip your port that he is now leaving.

Coachmen and guards were not paid very high wages, the Post Office only paying their guards 10s. a week; but on a popular coach the tips both received amounted to a considerable amount per annum. A Post Office guard would travel with his mail from seventy to eighty miles, and then a fresh guard would take his place; and with coachmen the same thing applied. The Edinburgh mail had twelve guards on the road.

Like their teams, they would go back the next night on the up mail, and "Broadback" returned to London on the following day on the mail which arrived at Thatcham at 12.30 a.m., he and his brother driving this stage on alternate nights.

The only drawback to this system was that these coachmen and guards had to keep up two homes; but, like sailors, who,

THE GEORGE AND PELICAN INN, NEWBURY.

I understand from nautical men, have a wife in every port, they may perhaps not have objected to this. I am afraid that some of my male friends who live at Maidenhead would queue up for the job to-day if a vacancy occurred. Like sailors, I don't suppose either guards or coachmen had such a very bad time, however much they may have grumbled to the Post Office and proprietors about the extra expense entailed.

Leaving the main street of Newbury on our left, the coach passed the celebrated George and Pelican Inn, a house where most of the

"SPRINGING THEM"

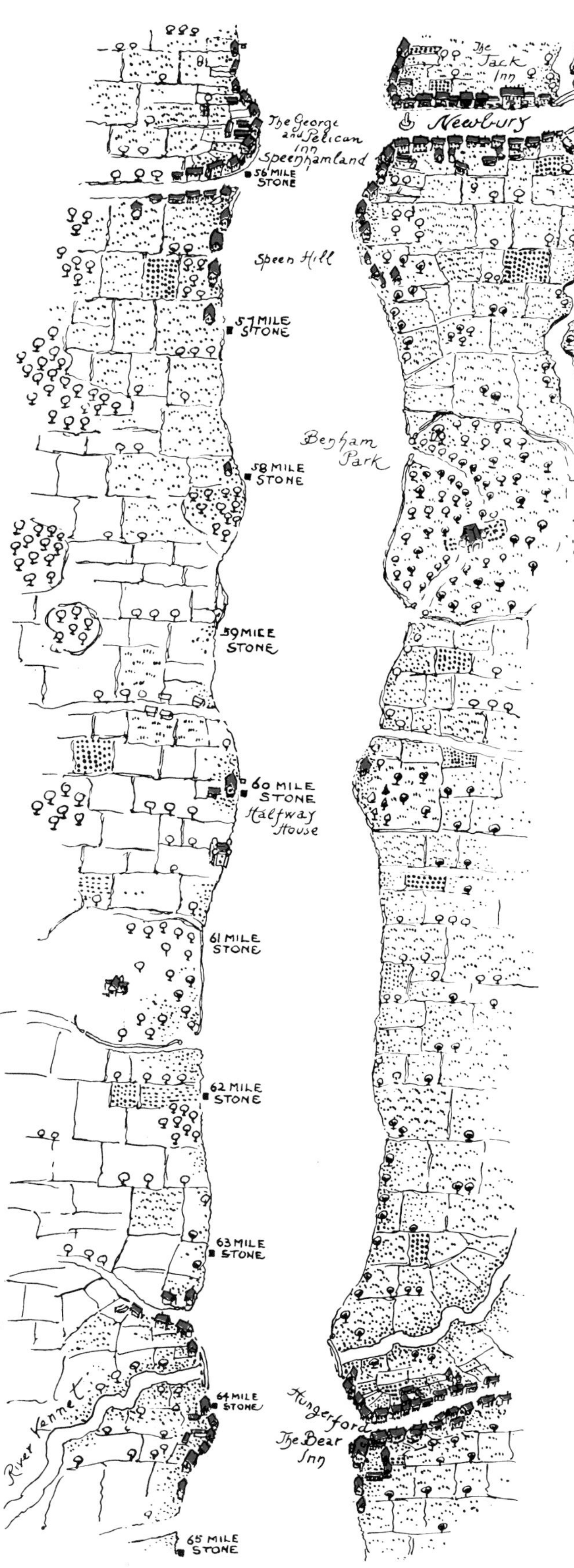

day coaches stopped and well known to every traveller on the Bath Road of that period.

> "The Pelican" at Speenhamland
> It stands upon a hill.
> You know it is "The Pelican"
> By its enormous bill,

quoted "Narrowback" as we passed by it, which may or may not have been a libel upon the landlady, the road-famous Mrs. Botham. A few miles from here the mail was driven past the old castellated toll-gates on the main road, which were erected in this form to mark the half-way spot between London and Bristol; at the time of our story Bristol was a very important seaport, and the Bristol Road had also the distinction of being the first southern road to be made under the able hands of Mr. Macadam. And then the road takes the travellers by the side of the Kennet, gleaming in the moonlight, to Hungerford Town and its Bear Inn.

This is a town of fisher-folk and tutti-men, a town of the rod and reel, where the nimble and elusive trout, disporting in the River Kennet, is tickled to death by disciples of Izaak Walton, and where tutti-men at Hock-tide kiss the girls who cannot pay.

The Halfway House between London and Bristol.

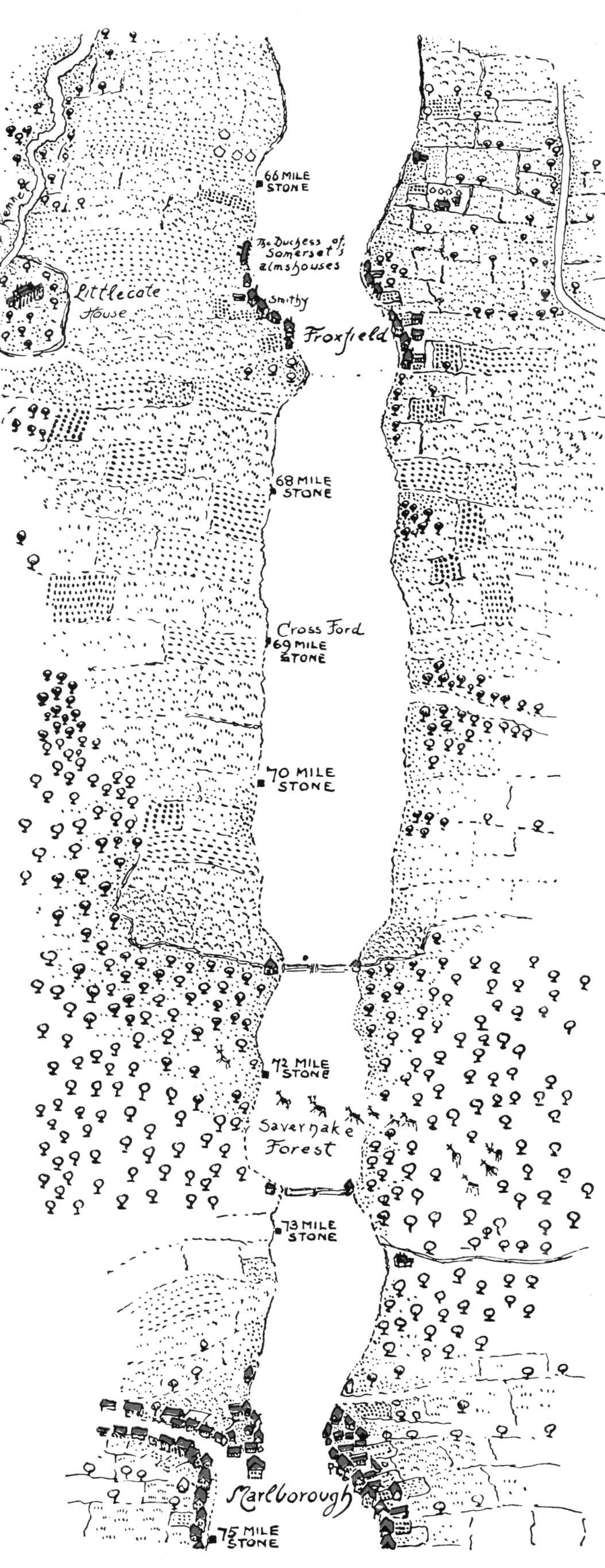

Unfortunately, I have no fishing story, neither have I personal experience of the tutti-man's art; and so we pass by Hungerford, "celebrated for its troutes," and the mail wheels roll on to the Duchess of Somerset's almshouses at Froxfield, where twenty-four clergymen's widows could live free.

As the morning sun rose behind the guard, "Narrowback" told the story of Littlecote Park, about a mile away, where once lived the notorious Wild Darrel or Dayrel.

The story goes that Dayrel, having "gott his lady's waiting-woman into trouble, sent a servant for a midwife who was to be brought to the house hoodwinked at the necessary time."

The child was born, but the "hoodwinked" midwife somehow or other raised her "hoodwink" and saw the cruel father "murther" the child and burn it in the fire!!!

The knowledge of this horrible deed so preyed upon her mind that she did her utmost to discover the house to which she had been taken when " hoodwinked." She conjectured it must have been some great house, as she had seen that the room in which the tragedy occurred was a very lofty one. Then, like a wise person, she went to a Justice of the Peace, a search was made, the chamber was found, and the " knight was brought to his tryall," all in correct story-book sequence. The result of the " tryall " was that Dayrel, for some unaccountable reason, was let off by a judge whose name was

POPHAM.

All of which took place in Queen Elizabeth's reign.

On consulting Patterson as the coach passed by in 1828, it was seen that

COLONEL POPHAM'S

address was Littlecote Park!!! Which, as " Broadback " commented, sounded appropriate to the purlieus of Hungerford—fishy.

And then in the early morning the glorious drive through Savernake or Marlborough Forest. The sun behind us threw long shadows from the coach and its team; but, unlike those cast by the setting sun when the mail set out, now acted as an advance guard instead of a rear guard.

A vixen with one of Farmer Giles's chickens in her jaws loped across the highway, making for the earth where her fast-growing family were awaiting their breakfast; a brace of magpies chattered at her as she rose on the opposite slope; a jay screeched spitefully as she passed under the tree where he was resting.

Rabbits stopped their breakfasts and scuttled back to their burrows, and a group of fallow deer stampeded at the sound of the approaching mail, which, leaving the forest behind, journeyed on to the entrance to the broad street of Marlborough, and pulled up at the Angel Inn for a fresh team of horses at 5.30 o'clock in the forenoon—according to the guard's time-sheet.

Here our coachman would allow a few minutes' wait, and then away once more up the High Street with its overhanging gables and delightful skyline, to the entrance to the Castle Inn.

This inn, as we know, is now part of Marlborough College, but it was in previous years the home of the Earl of Hertford.

Like many old houses, it had had its vicissitudes. It was built

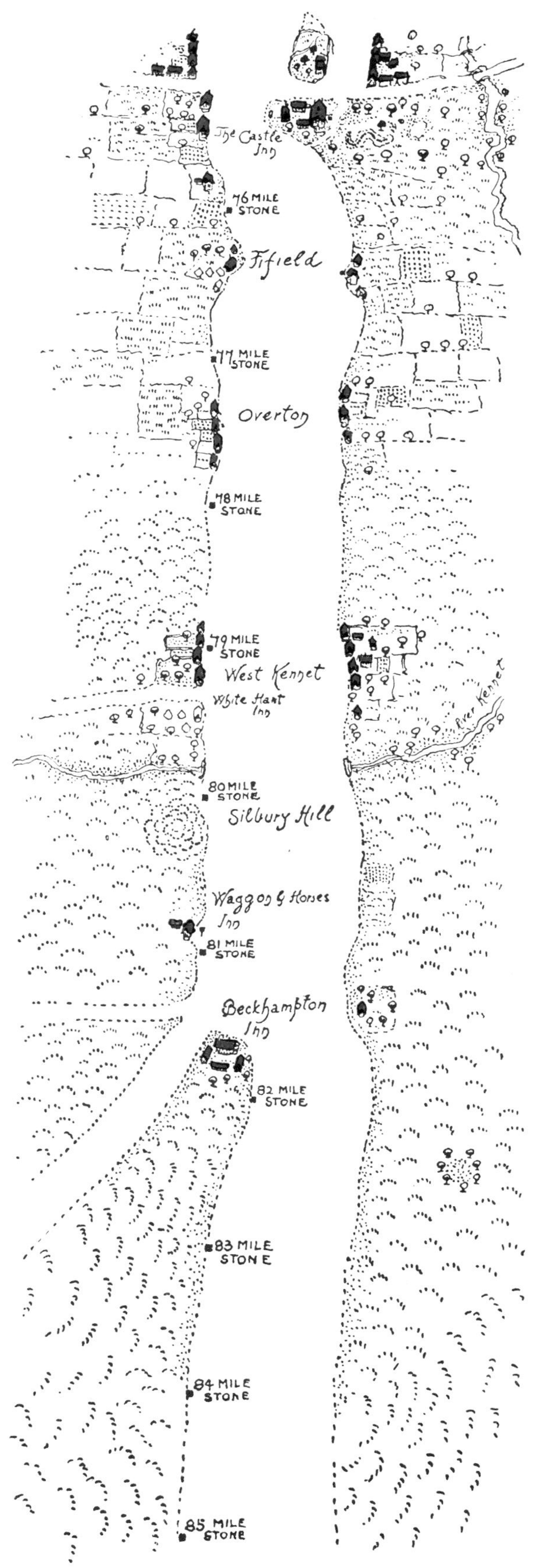

towards the end of the seventeenth century on the site of the then ruined Marlborough Castle, and Inigo Jones was responsible for its design but did not actually build it.

When erected for the Hertfords it was described as a "great rambling building," and had the fish-ponds, bowling green, clipped hedges and other "pleasaunces" which were the necessary adjuncts to a great family mansion of those days.

Lady Hertford, afterwards Duchess of Somerset, whose collection of clergymen's widows we have already passed at Froxfield, dearly loved her garden with its lawns surrounded by beehive-shaped yew trees, and here for some years after her husband's death she entertained the countryside and numerous literary and artistic notabilities.

On the death of her son the house passed, through her daughter, to the Duke of Northumberland, who, in the year 1757, allowed it to be turned into an inn, much to the disgust of the lady whose loving care had made its gardens so celebrated.

Apparently Mr. George Smith, of the Artillery Ground, London, was the first inn landlord, and it was also recorded that he was allowed to purchase some of the family portraits with the house, to the great horror of the friends of the Duchess, who recognized them later when they visited the inn.

The Castle Inn, as it was called, soon became a great hostelry on the Bath Road, perhaps the largest and most fashionable inn in England, and drew a very lucrative business for its proprietor for many years.

At the time our mail and her passengers passed it the landlord was Joseph White, and the house was then at the zenith of its fame as a coaching inn.

All through the daytime its approach was blocked with stage-coaches (forty coaches changed here daily), travelling carriages and post-chaises, for it was a favourite house for wealthy private individuals when travelling.

The Earl of Chatham, who always travelled *en prince*, was once kept a fortnight at this house owing to an attack of gout, and while there insisted on having the whole staff of the hostelry put into the Chatham livery in addition to his own servants.

During the winter months travellers to Bath were often forced to make a lengthened stay at Marlborough until the weather was suitable for crossing the much-dreaded Wiltshire Downs to Devizes, and when the comforts of the Castle Inn were available, they might have been loth to encounter snow, east winds or hail on the next two stages, much in the same way that a liable-to-be-seasick voyager hesitates to start across the Channel in rough weather.

The Castle Inn no doubt helped to give a considerable amount of prosperity to the town, until steam stepped in and heartlessly robbed it of all its glories.

The first change after leaving Marlborough was made at Beckhampton Inn. Along this part of the road at this early hour of the morning the ploughman might have been seen starting out with his team, the "fogger," and dairymaid going to the cattle sheds to milk the cows, for at that time there were no eight-hour days and the agricultural labourer made an early start.

Although, so far, no mention has been made of the guard, this important personality of the mail has since the coach left London had a great deal to do.

On the way his horn had to be constantly used, to get sleeping carters to move their teams from the crown of the road to allow the coach to pass, and also to warn the various Post Offices and sub-post stations to

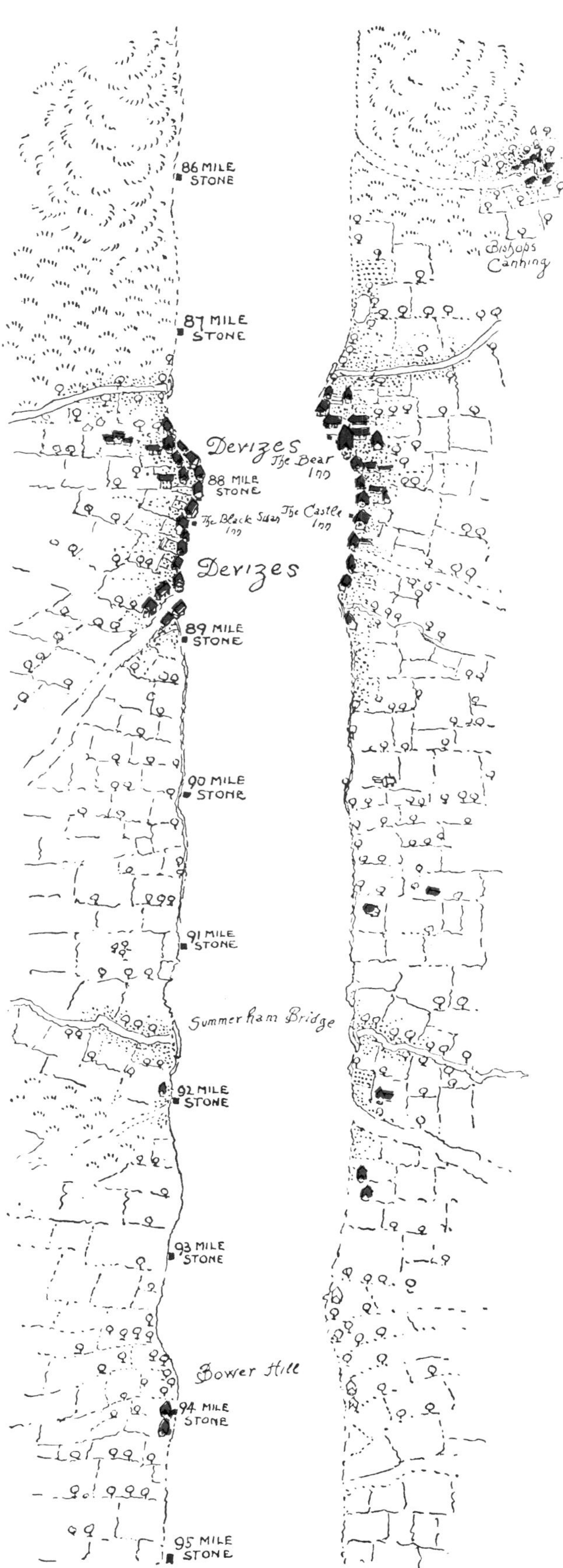

be in readiness to receive their mail-bags without causing the driver to lose valuable time.

Then also he would enliven the monotony of the drive through the night by playing selections on his key bugle. The "yard o' tin" was supplied to him by the Post Office, but his key bugle was his own private enterprise.

His favourite tunes were "Sally in our Alley," "The Post Horn Galop," etc.

Many of the stage-coach guards had fine voices, and a good song, well sung, no doubt increased the tip which was received when the passengers left the coach; moreover, a coach with a genial coachman and a cheery guard generally carried a *full house*.

As the guard sat alone on the back seat of the mail, the distance between the passengers and the vocalist might perhaps have given his efforts rather the effect of a screened and distant orchestra, and not necessarily have interfered with the flow of conversation.

Be that as it may, a guard's concert may not always have been welcome to inside passengers trying to sleep, although to those outside, where sleeping had its dangers, his music may have been more welcome.

I think it was De Quincey who found this singing by the guard rather an overrated pastime—but he may have been unlucky in his performer, or have been suffering from indigestion.

A Village Post Office.

On arrival at the change the guard helped with it, if he had no mails to attend to and deliver—so that less than every hour he had to get down from his perch and do some work which would stretch his stiffened limbs.

Besides this he had mail-bags to leave at many points on the road which were not changing places. Sometimes, to a waiting Post

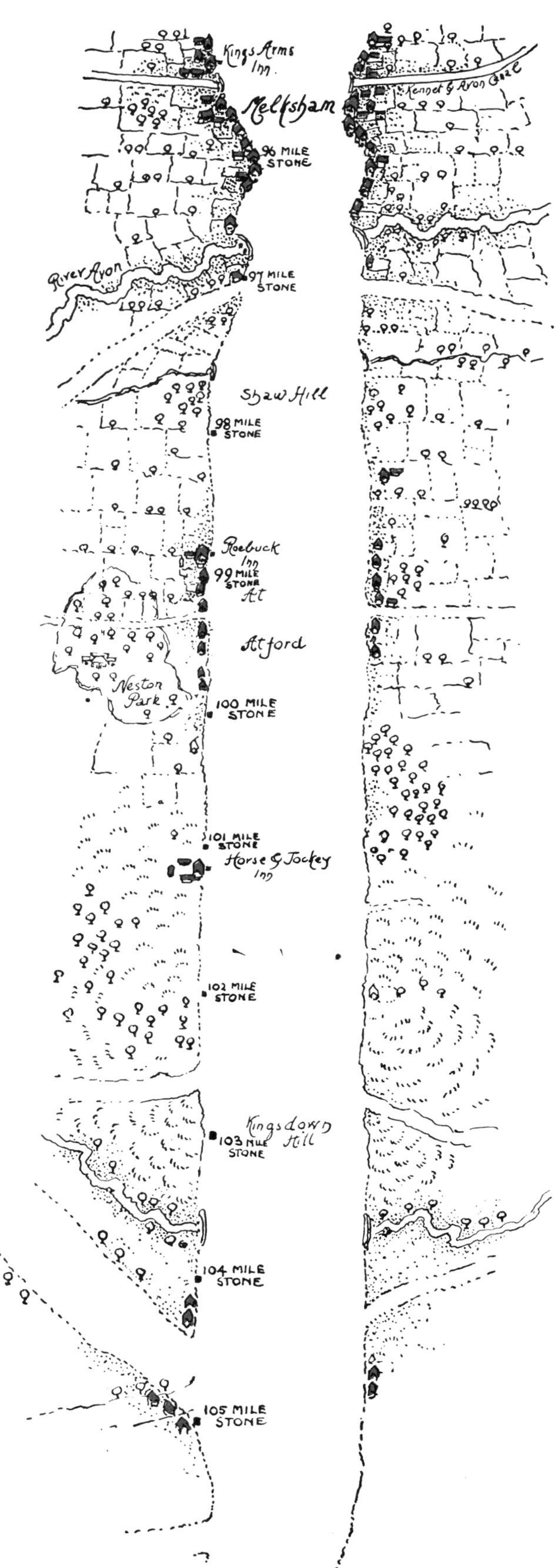

Office messenger; at other times they were passed through the bedroom window of the village postmaster, whose night-capped head would appear at the open lattice, while the coach wheels hardly stopped revolving.

A long pole, or shepherd's crook, with its hook on the end was occasionally used for this purpose, the guard taking off the down or up mails, as the case might be, and replacing this with the bag for the village and surrounding district.

A mail guard's first duty was to deliver his mails whatever the weather conditions. Snow, hail or fog, he had to get them to their destination.

In the hard snowstorms of December '36, many guards had terribly trying experiences.

Mail-coaches were buried in snowdrifts all over England, coaches had to be abandoned and guards had to ride on alone with the mail-bags tied on their horse's backs, while the unfortunate passengers were left to get themselves out of the snowdrifts as best they could; about which we will tell later when we join the Portsmouth Road for a winter day's travel, only here stating that our Thatcham coachman remembered the great snowstorm of 1808, when Neville, the guard at that time, was found frozen to death on arrival at Devizes; and just as the driver finished the story the mail drove up to the Black Bear Inn at that town at 6.50 o'clock in the forenoon on this summer's morning.

"Passed through the Bedroom Window of the Village Postmaster."

Devizes in the early part of the nineteenth century was celebrated for its cloth factories, and was a very important and populous town.

The two most important of its inns were "The Bear" and "The Castle," at both of which post-boys were always ready to drive the traveller; the former building was a picturesque and rambling old house with large stables at the back.

At the Bear Inn the mail changed horses, the twelfth team on the road, and the way in which this change was made I should like to describe. To take four horses successfully out of a coach and harness four fresh ones in their places, in the space of one minute and a-half or two minutes, was an operation which had to be done like clockwork with everything in correct order.

When the change was in sight and the guard had sounded the notes on his horn to warn the ostlers to be in readiness, the coachman asked the passenger beside him to unbuckle the ends of the lead and wheel reins just before the mail came to a standstill.

"Nimrod," in the *Sporting Magazine* of two years before, had commented upon these very rapid changes, then in vogue on the road, and I cannot do better than quote so able an authority:

"There is no part of coaching economy in which a greater alteration has been made than in the act of changing horses.

"It scarcely seems credible that four horses can be taken from a coach, and four others put into their places, in the very short space of sixty seconds; but so it is.

"A quarter of an hour, or at least ten minutes, was the usual time allowed for this purpose when I first knew the road; but at the present day, unless some business is to be transacted such as taking fares for passengers, setting down, getting out parcels, etc., I should say the average is three minutes for each change, with fast coaches.

"There is, however, one practice attending this harlequin-like performance which I must condemn, and which I would not suffer if I were the proprietor of the fastest coach in England. That is—having no buckles at the end of either leaders' or wheelers' reins, for should one of them drop out of the coachman's hands, it would be out of his power to recover it, and an accident must be the consequence."

Another authority, but of a little later period, gives the following as the best method of negotiating the change:

"A smart coachman usually took his place in changing horse, and it was quite possible, as I know from experience, having been timed by a box passenger, to effect the change in one minute and a-half, with only one horsekeeper, assisted by coachman and guard; but to do this every one must know his own place; they must not be tumbling over one another. The best drill I ever knew for this purpose was as follows: As the coach gradually stopped, the guard got down and ran forward to unhook the near leader's outside trace, and then drew the lead rein through the terrets, after which he changed the near horse, and finished by running the near lead rein; the horsekeeper, on the offside, unhooked the remaining lead traces, uncoupled the wheel horses, and changed the offside one. The coachman, getting down as fast as he could, finished changing the leaders.

"The horses had, of course, previous to the arrival of the coach, been properly placed, the wheel on each side of the road and the leaders coupled."

There is very little doubt, however, that there were many ways of performing this operation—one equally as good as the other, although each coachman may have had his own pet theory.

Over the Kennet and Avon Canal the mail travelled into Melksham, another cloth factory town, where a group of children awaited her at the side of the road. These bare-legged and unshod imps, both girls and boys, made a practice of meeting many of the coaches during the day and, by running by the side of them and turning cartwheels as they went, collected quite a lot of money for their parents from the coppers thrown to them by the passengers.

Calne, on the other Bath Road, was more notorious for this practice than Melksham, and Pierce Egan, in his *Walks Through Bath*, 1828, said of them, "the girls keeping tight hold of petticoats and tumbling over head and heels with the greatest ease and agility, and on quitting the coach they immediately lay themselves down at the side of the road till another coach appeared and so on till end of day." (Quite a strenuous day for girls, I should imagine.)

This pastime, which a few years ago, on Derby Day and Ascot week, used to be a common one among gipsy children, in 1828 seems to have been a perquisite of Wiltshire, and more especially of the towns in the vicinity of Bath.

Then one last change and the coach ran on down Kingsdown Hill, and at 8.15 a.m. the mail rattled through Walcot turnpike and entered the City of Bath.

At 8.20 she delivered her mails at the Post Office, and set down her passengers, and so came to the end of her journey.

In the city the chief coaching inns were the "Lamb," "White Lion," "White Hart," and York Hotel; and the "White Hart" stood where we now see the Royal Pump Room hostelry. The last two on the list had most of the coaching traffic.

THE WHITE HART INN (NOW ROYAL PUMP ROOM HOTEL), BATH.

Much of Bath to-day is as it was when my puppets journeyed its road; much the same as when Charles Dickens wrote about it, or when Beau Nash held sway in it—as the arbiter of fashion. Pump Room, terraces, courts and alleys, all breathe out an atmosphere of the eighteenth and early nineteenth centuries, and as we walk through the old city we can easily see our fellow-passengers of the Bath mail traversing its streets.

"Narrowback" raises his hat to us; and "Gentlemen, we leave you here," from guard and coachman, reminds us that the journey is finished, and that we have returned to 1928 with its motor traction, railways, aeroplanes, telegraph, telephones, and wireless; and our own journey in the Bath mail, "at the incredibly fast rate of travel" of 11 miles an hour, has come to an end.

H.R.H. Duke of Kent, Kensington Palace Lord Holland, Holland House	Kensington	
A. Copeland, Esq. Major Morrison	Turnham Green	Duke of Devonshire, Chiswick House Hon. Col. Cavendish, Sutton Court Mrs. Louth, Grove House
Col. Clitheroe, Boston House	Brentford	Duke of Northumberland, Syon House
E. Ellice, Esq., Wyke House Earl of Jersey, Osterley Park Lady Banks, Spring Grove	Smallbury Green	R. Hope, Esq. Lord J. Hay, Worton House E. C. Southbrook, Esq., Worton Lodge H. Cerf, Esq., Worton Hall
Countess of Berkeley, Cranford Park	Cranford Bridge	
Rt. Hon. John Sullivan Richings J. Boswell, Esq., Iver Lodge Lord Gambier, Iver Grove	Colnbrook	Lord Montague, Ditton Park
Sir R. B. Harvey, Bart., Langley Park J. Jackson, Esq., Langley Lodge Mrs. Buckland, Langley Grove	Slough	Sir W. Johnson, Bart., Burnham Grove
J. Penn, Esq., Stoke Park Lord Sefton, Stoke Farm Rev. Evans, Britwell House	Salt Hill	
Pascoe Grenfell, Esq., Taplow House Lord Newry, Berry Hill T. Lucas, Esq., Taplow Hill Mrs. Tunno, Taplow Lodge	Maidenhead Bridge	T. Wilson, Esq., Ives Place Sir W. Herne
Sir G. Warrinder, Bart., Cliefden Sir S. Young, Formosa Place	Maidenhead	Mrs. A. M. Trenchard, Hendons House W. Dodwell, Esq., Knibers
Lord Boston, Hedsor Lodge Lord Grenville, Dropmore Mrs. Hall, The Enns T. Atkinson, Esq., The Cottage Col. Brotherton Stubbings Sir Gilbert East, Bart., Hall Place Gen. Vansittart, Bisham Abbey	Maidenhead Thicket	C. Sawyer, Esq., Altwood T. Althorpe, Esq., Bullocks Hatch H. Harford, Esq., Down Place H. Walter, Esq., Holyport C. Fuller, Esq., Philberts W. Atkins, Esq., Braywick Grove Mrs. E. Law, Cannon Hill Admiral West, Braywick Lodge A. Vansittart, Shottesbrook Park
Mrs. Cavendish, Bear Hill Sir Morris Ximenes, Bear Place	Hare Hatch	John Kearney, Esq., White Waltham C. Corneford, Esq., Waltham Place Mrs. Lee Perrott, Scarlets
Dr. Phillimore, Shiplake House Lord Mark Ker, Holme Wood R. Palmer, Esq., Holme Park Col. Marsac, Caversham Park	Twyford	Lady Sherbourn, Ruscombe House Sir John Lloyd Dukenfield, Bart., Stanlake House Lady Eyre, Hurst Park Mrs. Wowen, Hurst House

	Twyford	J. Wheble, Esq., Woodley Lodge Lord Sidmouth, Early Court E. Golding, Esq., Maiden Early
Mrs. Liebenrood, Prospect Park Mrs. Beville, Calcot House Col. Blagrave, Tilehurst Place	Reading	Duke of Wellington, Strathfieldsaye Park B. Monck, Coley Park
R. P. Benyon de Beauvoir, Esq., Englefield House	Theal	Mrs. Thoyts, Sulhampstead House Sir C. S. Hunter, Bart., Mortimer Hill
Rev. C. Stephens, Bradfield Hall	Jack's Booth	C. Brockhurst, Esq., Oakfield Park T. Bacon, Esq., Padworth House W. Congreve, Esq., Aldermaston House W. Mount, Esq., Wasing House
Earl of Falmouth, Woolhampton House W. Poyntz, Esq., Midgham House B. Bunbury, Esq., Marlston House	Woolhampton	
Dr. Penrose, Shaw House F. S. Stead, Esq., Donnington Castle House J. Bebb, Esq., Donnington Grove	Newbury	Mrs. Williams, Speen Lawn Mrs. Parry, Donnington Priory Margravine of Anspach, Benham Place Earl of Craven, Hampstead Lodge
Fulwar Craven, Esq., Chilton House G. H. Cherry, Esq., Denford House Gen. Popham, Littlecot Park	Hungerford	J. Willes, Esq., Hungerford Park Mrs. Shaw, Inglewood House
Sir Francis Burdett, Bart., Ramsbury Manor	Marlborough	Marquis of Aylesbury, Savernake Lodge John Goodman, Esq., Oare House Admiral Sir G. Montague, Stowell Lodge
	Fyfield	Mrs. Watkin, Lockeridge House
	Overton	R. Matthews, Esq., Overton House
T. G. Bucknell Estcourt, Esq., New Park	Devizes	W. Salmon, Esq., South Broom House
	Summerham Bridge	T. Burges, Esq., Seend Lodge Ambrose Audrey, Esq., Seend
	Melksham	
Mrs. Heathcote, Shaw Hill House Mrs. Dickenson, Monks House	Shaw	Admiral Sir Harry Neale, Bart., Shaw House
R. Fowler, Esq., Chapel House	Atford	J. B. Hale, Esq., Cottles House
J. Wiltshire, Esq., Shockerwick	Kingsdown Hill	D. J. Long, Esq., Monkton Farley H. Skrine, Esq., Warley House
	Bathford	John Wiltshire, Esq., Bathford House
G. Adams, Esq., Bailbrook House	Bath Easton	C. Penoyre, Esq., Bath Easton Villa
	Bath	W. Thomas, Esq., Prior Park G. Tugwell, Esq., Crow Hall

The PORTSMOUTH ROAD

Once more the clocks of Piccadilly had struck the hour of eight, but on this occasion it was upon a cold morning in December instead of a warm evening in July; a morning certainly not calculated to inspire Londoners with a desire to travel the country on the outside of a stage-coach. Snow had fallen over the town during the night and had rapidly turned to slush in the streets, and the Portsmouth up mail, half an hour late at the Post Office, had reported a heavy fall on many parts of the road.

On this morning, in the year eighteen hundred and twenty-eight, the " Regulator," stage-coach to Portsmouth Town, had left her yard at the " Bolt-in-Tun," Fleet Street, in the gloom of a London fog. Link-boys with torches had accompanied her as far as the "Golden Cross" at Charing Cross, as she slowly felt her way to her point of departure from London, Hatchett's " White Horse Cellars " in Piccadilly.

Other stage-coaches had already set out for the same seaport and had left their various yards with similar escorts; the earlier and slower conveyances having started from London by the true Portsmouth road, crossing over London Bridge, instead of following the route by which the " Regulator "—fast coach—left town.

We, on this journey to Portsmouth—in this *Romance of the Road* —travelled by the " Regulator," only leaving her now for a short time at her Piccadilly stop, while we journey a few miles of the road on one of the slower stages which crossed over London Bridge and plodded its way through the Borough, Newington, Vauxhall, and Wandsworth Village.

Butchers' shops and inns, the former all on the west, and the latter on the east side, were the chief features of the Borough High Street at that time, but at neither "The George" nor the ancient Tabard Inn did this slow coach on that morning pick up passengers.

Past the Marshalsea Prison, the temporary home of debtors and for those indicted for piracy on the high seas, this "rumble-tumble" stage-coach slowly splashed her way, leaving behind her the King's Bench Prison, whose inmates (if able to pay for it) might procure permission to walk in the snow in St. George's Fields.

Through Newington and Vauxhall turnpikes to Battersea Rise, dropping down to Wandsworth and crossing the Wandle River, and so past Howitt's Farm (the corner here being then known as Howitt's Corner), up the rise to the Obelisk and then on to Putney Heath.

Roque's map, made fifty years before, shows Howitt's Farm as the only house between Wandsworth Village and the Halfway House adjoining Kingston Gate; no wonder in those days that Putney's lonely heath was the home of footpads and highwaymen.

When my stage-coaches travelled to Portsmouth the highwayman was almost extinct, and even the footpad had but a precarious foothold in this neighbourhood.

Putney Obelisk, at the beginning of the heath, was erected in 1776 to David Hartley, who had invented (so every one believed) a method of making upper storeys of houses fireproof when a fire raged below, and George III and Queen Charlotte, we are told, breakfasted without inconvenience in a room in his fire-house at Putney when the building was burning beneath them.

A sum of over £2,000 was voted by Parliament to the inventor to carry on his experiments, but to-day the Obelisk is apparently the only result of his labours, and, as a work of art, it appears to be hardly worth the money.

From here the stage-coaches from London Bridge travelled the heath road to Robin Hood turnpike gate, but just before they approached it the apex of a triangle was reached, as at this point the "Rocket," "Regulator," and other fast coaches from Piccadilly

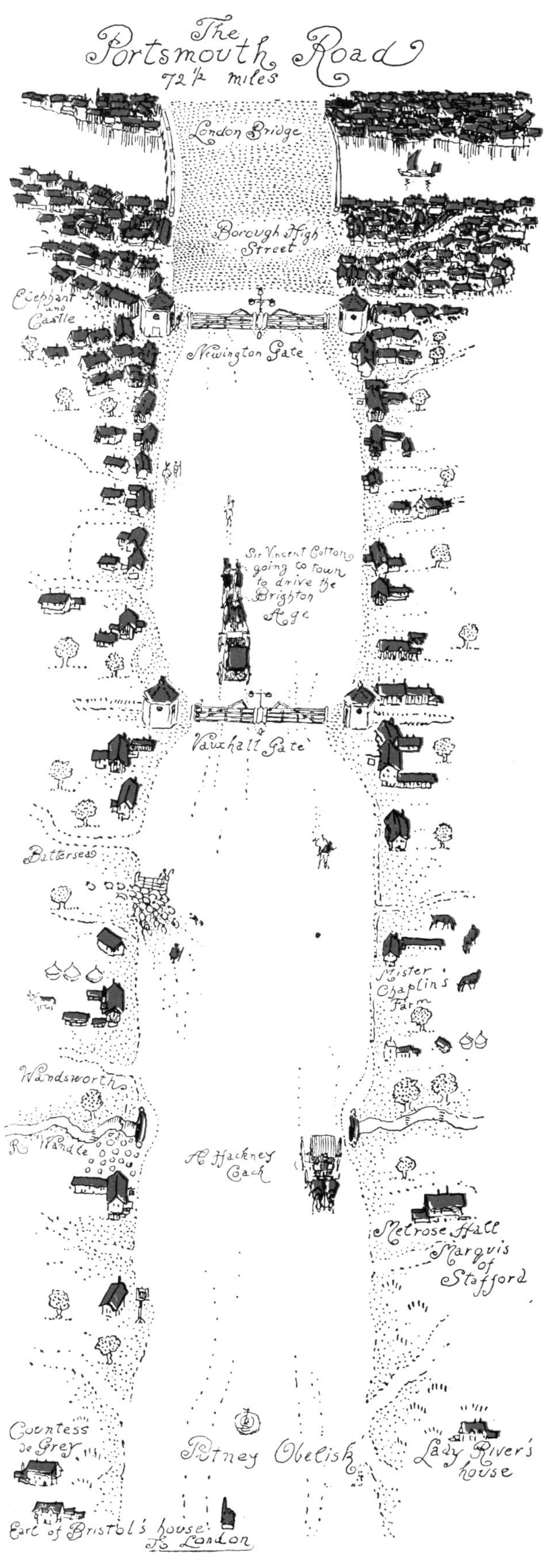

would join issue with the slow coaches from London Bridge on the true Portsmouth Road.

And now we will return to the "White Horse Cellars," where the "Regulator's" coachman has given the "All right, let 'em go" to the ostlers and the loin cloths have been whisked off the horses' backs.

To-day one can scarcely realize the bustle and movement which took place each morning at the two chief Piccadilly coaching houses, between the hours of seven and ten o'clock.

The mails, as we know, all started at eight o'clock at night. But in the morning stage-coaches for all parts of the West of England as well as for Portsmouth set out from one or other of them. It is not easy to visualize ten, or twenty, four-horse coaches standing, starting, or pulling up outside their doors, when the only time most of us have ever seen a four-in-hand is at one of the Horse Shows; yet this scene was a daily occurrence in 1828 between the hours mentioned.

From ten or eleven onwards only the ordinary traffic filled Piccadilly, but in the evening, between six and seven, the dusty and mud-splashed up coaches began to arrive, while at a few minutes to eight the spick-and-span mails drove up to collect mails and passengers for their nightly drive.

The Portsmouth stage-coaches for the first half-mile of their journey, i.e. from Hatchett's to Knightsbridge Corner, poached upon the Bath Road's preserves, starting on the same road that the mails "Devonport," "Exeter," "Bath," and "Gloucester" took in the evening at the same hour.

We know that portion of the road; we have already been down it when travelling to Bath.

We know where Tattersall's yard stood, and that the gates at Hyde Park Corner had only just been erected; so we may pass along it down the Brompton Road, where our stage-coach leaves it, until we reach the point where South Kensington to-day rears its solid ugliness in front of us.

A few houses, but mostly market gardens and nurseries, lined this part of the highway which passed down Bell Lane (Brompton Road) to the Queen's Elm, a tree standing by itself on the roadside. And so the Portsmouth stage-coach travelled on by Chelsea Park and little Chelsea Village almost to Parson's Green, to Putney's wooden bridge, to cross over which the coaches paid an eighteenpenny toll.

But Putney or Fulham Old Bridge (four miles from London) deserves a picture—

Putney Old Bridge.

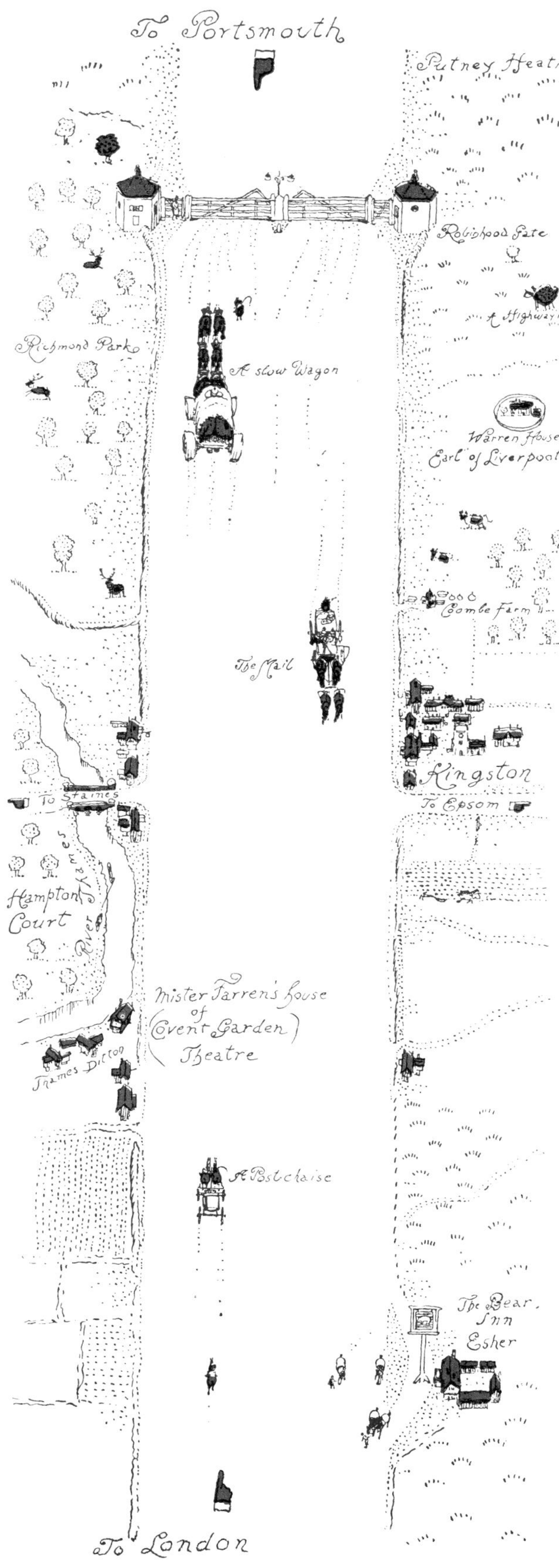

It was constructed by "Mr. Philips," carpenter to King George II, and rather looks like it—anyhow it was certainly a carpenter's job and not a bridge-builder's.

After this, up the rise to Putney Heath, until two miles farther on the journey, the apex of our triangle was once more reached near the Halfway House at Kingston Vale.

Putney one hundred years ago was not the populous suburb that it is now, but a fashionable neighbourhood; Earl Bathurst, the Earl of Bristol, Viscount Clifden, Lady Grantham and many others of the peerage had country houses there, and near David Hartley's fire-house was Bowling Green House, which at one time belonged to William Pitt, and in which house he died in 1806.

Bowling Green House had been built on the site of a mansion of the same name, celebrated as a fashionable resort for public breakfasts and assemblies; and no doubt, in the latter part of the eighteenth century, the smart thing to do was to drive down to Putney for breakfast.

The house of Edward Gibbon, the historian, faced Putney Heath just at the point where the stage-coaches climbing Putney Hill reached the common, so that

Putney had about that time many distinguished people living in its "salubrious purlieus."

Roque, in his map, marks the Gibbon ancestral home, and Edward Gibbon knew old Putney Bridge well, as Lyson tells us that as far back as he (Gibbon) could remember the house near the bridge, then the residence of his grandfather, Mr. James Porter, was the one where most of his holidays were spent.

On the morning the "Regulator" stage-coach travelled across Putney Heath the Gibbon family mansion did not look a very pleasant place to take up one's residence, and we can quite understand why young Gibbon preferred his grandfather's home in the neighbourhood of Putney's fascinating wooden bridge and the alluring playground of the banks of the River Thames to the bleak and dreary outlook from the paternal residence.

As the "Regulator" travelled this snow-covered common and sunk the dip towards Robin Hood Gate, her few outside passengers pulled mufflers and coats tighter around their shivering bodies, and the white landscape recalled to mind among them many experiences of previous snow-storms; times when mail-coaches had to be abandoned, when guards rode on with the mail-bags, when stage-coaches disappeared in snow-drifts, and when travellers were held prisoners at wayside inns and farmhouses until the snow-covered turnpike roads again became passable for horse traffic.

Most of these reminiscences were of the great frost of 1814—the year when an ox was roasted whole on the frozen Thames—but it was in 1836 that coach travellers, guards and coachmen had to experience one of the worst series of snow-storms on record. Then, for more than a week, every turnpike road in England was buried feet deep in snow, and the great Duke of Wellington, when travelling to attend a wedding at Badminton, had to have his chaise-and-four dug out on the Marlborough Downs. So many are the records and incidents of the snow-storm of that Christmastide that it will be interesting for us to recall some of them.

In contemporary news-sheets we read that a few days before the Christmas of '36 many coaches left London drawn by eight horses; but the heavy snow-storm started in earnest on Christmas night, a

Saturday, and the up mails all arrived late at St. Martin's-le-Grand on Sunday morning in consequence.

On arrival at the Post Office on this Sunday, "Glasgow's" guard reported the northern roads very deeply covered in snow, and that on some parts of the mail route it had taken two hours to do four miles.

"Exeter" was nearly three hours late with the news that snow around Dorchester had drifted to five feet in depth, and "Devonport" (the "Quicksilver") did not get to St. Martin's-le-Grand until 11.30 a.m.—her time of arrival being 6.48 at normal times—having taken thirty hours to do the 217 miles which she was scheduled to do in twenty-four hours and forty-five minutes!!!

"Going On with the Mails."

All of which does not sound very terrible to us to-day, but which at that time, when mails were never one minute late and when we set our watches by them in the country, would mean very serious accidents or, as in this case, a fall of snow of exceptional severity.

The guard of the "Quicksilver," who had come from Ilminster (140 miles), said that the bad storm commenced at Wincanton and continued until London was reached; that between Andover and Whitchurch the north wind blowing snow and sleet in their faces almost blinded them; that the mail stuck fast in a snow-drift; that the horses were buried; and that the coachman on getting down also disappeared. Luckily a wagon and four horses came up, and with the help of these they were able to restart the coach. However, all trace of the mail route was by this time obliterated, and the coachman had to continue his journey by guess-work and by trusting to the instinct of his horses.

On the Monday, "Portsmouth" seemed to have had less trouble than most of the mails, at any rate on the earlier stages of her journey; and this was partly due to much of the route lying high and the wind blowing the snow as it fell off the crown of the road. After passing Guildford, snow-drifts began seriously to impede their travelling, making their arrival at the Post Office two hours late.

"Holyhead" and "Chester" both got into trouble near Dunstable, the former falling into a snow-drift and only being extricated after great difficulty, and the latter having to be entirely abandoned and her mails transferred to the "Holyhead" coach, using the eight horses to continue her journey.

On Tuesday, in consequence of the non-arrival of so many mails, the Post Office authorities began to have serious trouble in order to find guards for the outgoing coaches. All supernumerary guards were called up, and even strangers were sworn in to travel on the guard's perch in charge of the mail bags. Regular guards who came in that afternoon on the up mails were forced to go out again at eight o'clock.

Both the Bath and Bristol mails had to be abandoned eighty miles from London on this Tuesday, the mail bags being sent on across country in a chaise and four with the two guards, who arrived in London on Wednesday morning at 6 a.m.

Numbers of mails and stage-coaches were left to their fate in the snow between Slough and Maidenhead, which seems to have been one of the worst parts of the Bath Road.

Another Bristol coach, which should have arrived in London on Monday the 26th at 7.30 p.m., did not get to town until Tuesday at midday, and our friend the Portsmouth "Regulator" was buried on

"The Road was Strewn with Abandoned Mails, Coaches, and Post-chaises."

Horndean Hill for nearly four hours, and only an army of farm men and horses after much time and labour were able to pull her out.

Some of these custodians of His Majesty's mails performed prodigies of endurance during that week, showing true British bulldog tenacity in carrying out their duties, and upholding the traditions of the Post Office service; but a mail-guard's own description of what he went through at that time is the best evidence of this, and for that reason we will hear what Nobbs, the guard of the Exeter Old Mail, had to say about his journey as related by F. E. Baines, Inspector-General of Mails, in his book *Forty Years at the Post Office.*

"After leaving Bristol at seven o'clock," Nobbs stated, "all went well until we were nearing Salisbury—that is to say, about midnight. Snow had been falling for some time before, but after leaving Salisbury it came down so thick, and lay so deep, that we were brought to a standstill, and found it impossible to proceed any further. Consequently we had to leave the coach and proceed on horseback to the next changing-place, where I took a fresh horse and started for Southampton. There I procured a chaise and pair and continued my journey to Portsmouth, arriving there at 6 p.m. the next day. I was then ordered to go back to Bristol. On reaching Southampton on my return journey the snow had got much deeper, and at Salisbury I found that the London mails had not arrived. I could not proceed any further. Not to be 'done' [there is an example for our present-day chauffeurs—AUTHOR] I took a horse out of the stable, slung the mail bags over his back and pushed on for Bristol, where I arrived next day after much wandering through fields, up and down lanes, across country all one dreary expanse of snow.

By this time I was about ready for a rest; but there was no rest for me in Bristol, for I was ordered by the Mail Inspector to take the mails on to Birmingham, as there was no other guard available.

At last I arrived at Birmingham, having been on duty for two days and nights continuously without taking off my clothes."

When one remembers that all of this took place during one of the worst snow-storms of the century, and that the distance from Bristol to Portsmouth and back is 198 miles and from Bristol to Birmingham eighty-eight miles, making a total of 286 miles in deep snow, Nobbs's achievement is marvellous.

To continue the diary of this snow-storm of 1836, on Wednesday, the 28th, the roads became impassable for wheeled traffic, and the country was strewn with abandoned mails, stage-coaches, and post-chaises.

Near St. Albans the Liverpool mail, when deep in a snow-drift, found two ladies in an abandoned post-chaise, the post-boys having gone on to St. Albans to try to procure fresh horses.

The up mails outside St. Albans were completely blocked by drifts, 300 soldiers being called out (sappers and miners) to dig them out and make a passage for them into the town, when the letters were sent on with the guards only by post-chaise to London.

On Thursday, the 29th, more and more snow fell, things on the highways became even worse, and the Dover mail was only able to get as far as Rochester. No communication either by horse or foot beyond this town had been possible for some days, and at Chatham snow was reported from thirty to forty feet deep. The Surveyor of Roads applied to the military authorities of that town for help, and 600 soldiers were called out to clear a way through.

Seventeen coaches on the northern route were stuck fast in the snow at Dunstable, near Coventry, and similar experiences to the drivers of every kind of conveyance happened all over the country.

On Monday, the 26th, a correspondent from Brighton gave the following report: "All this part of the country is at the present moment buried in snow. A stable-man was picked up in Black Lion Street frozen to death. The 'Times' coach, which leaves London at four o'clock and generally arrives here a little after nine, did not get in on Monday night until twenty minutes past eleven, being for the last fifteen miles of the journey clogged up with snow. The Gloucester mail, which ought to have been in by five o'clock, was obliged to stop on the road, and the guard and coachman reached this town only at one o'clock in the morning, having brought the bags in a cart along the beach; they were, however, so affected by the cold that the guard now lies, it is feared, in a dying state.

The mail started as usual for London on Monday night, but had not got three miles before it was obliged to return.

A King's Messenger, who had important dispatches with him, attempted, with the assistance of a guide, to travel on horseback, but could not get on and," the account adds, " the Messenger is about to start again in a post-chaise, and the mail bags will go with him, but no passengers.

Not a coach besides has left this town or come into it."

And so on and so forth, the same thing happening in every part of England.

I have given rather a large amount of space to this 1836 snow-storm week because I want you to realize what travelling on the " Regulator " to Portsmouth in wintry weather was like in the year 1828, when guards might be frozen to death in their seats, and even passengers killed by the cold.

But when we temporarily abandoned her to make this detour of the mail-historic-Christmastide of 1836 she was crossing Putney Heath.

Robin Hood Inn was in sight when this stage-coach joined the Portsmouth Road, and here it was that her first change of horses stood waiting, and her first toll-gate straddled the road ahead.

" The Change."

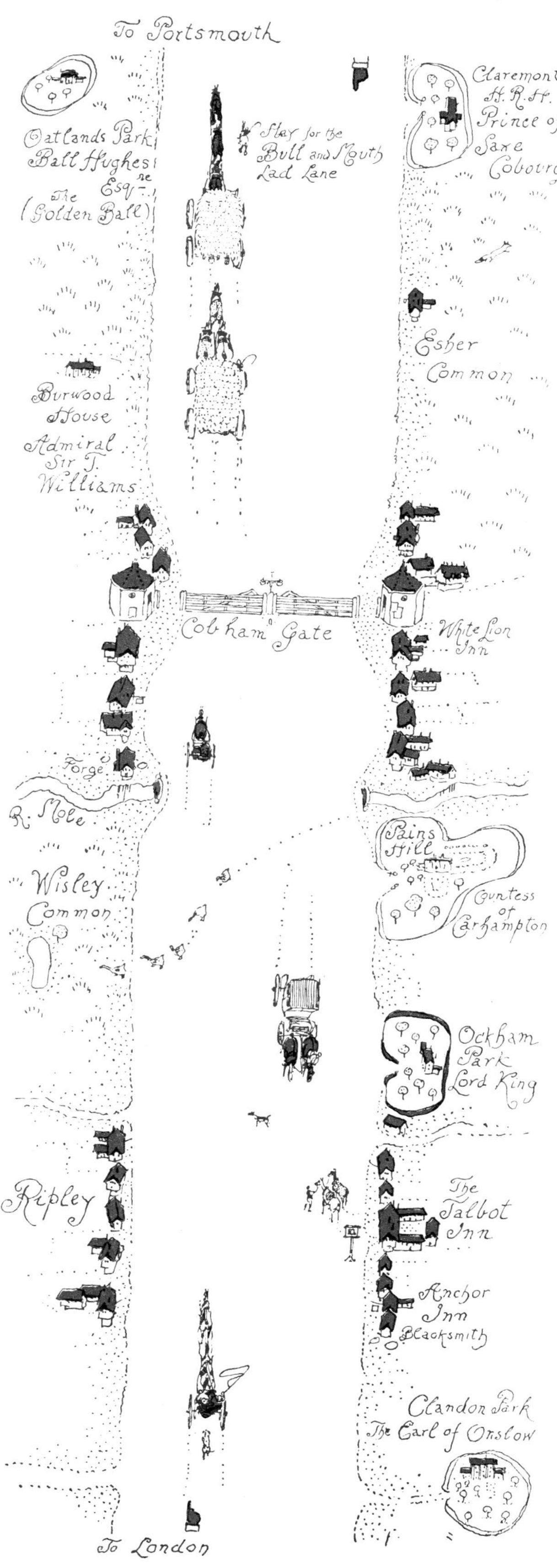

Although stage-coaches kept to their scheduled time-tables as far as possible, it was by the mails that the inhabitants of England set their watches, and in changing horses the speed of the change as accomplished on the night mails was not attempted or expected on the ordinary stage-coaches.

Travellers on these liked to have a few moments in which to get refreshment, or to get down and stretch their limbs, and did not wish to be hustled away again almost before the coach had come to a standstill.

The "Regulator" was a fast coach, but not like Sir Vincent Cotton's "Brighton Age," or, rather, the coach which Sir Vincent drove as amateur coachman.

In my first little map of the Portsmouth Road you can see him journeying to town in his four-horse travelling chariot for this purpose. The "Age" changed horses at the same rapid pace as the rest of the journey was accomplished, and so also did a few of the very fastest stage-coaches; but it was the exception rather than the rule, and time-tables (including stoppages) generally allowed five or six minutes for the change.

After passing through Robin Hood Gate the coach passed

FIVE MINUTES FOR REFRESHMENTS

Warren House, and the Earl of Liverpool's property was on the Coombe Farm side. In Richmond Park could be seen Great Lodge where Lieut.-Gen. Sir Henry Campbell lived, and also New Lodge, the house of Lord Sidmouth.

From here the "Regulator" travelled through Kingston Market Square and then followed the Thames past Mr. Farren's house ("of Covent Garden Theatre," according to Patterson—no doubt a little bit of gratuitous publicity), over Ditton Marsh to the Bear Inn at Esher, where her second fresh team stood ready by the side of the road. "The Bear," or "The Brown Bear," as it was originally called, was a changing-place for many of the coaches. After this, Claremont Gates were left behind on the near side of the road, in which house lived at that time H.R.H. the Prince of Saxe-Coburg.

On Ditton Marsh, where the road was not hedged, the heavy fall of snow had made it none too easy for the "Regulator's" coachman to proceed—the milestones and previous wheel-tracks being the only marks for his guidance.

"None Too Easy for the Coachman to Proceed."

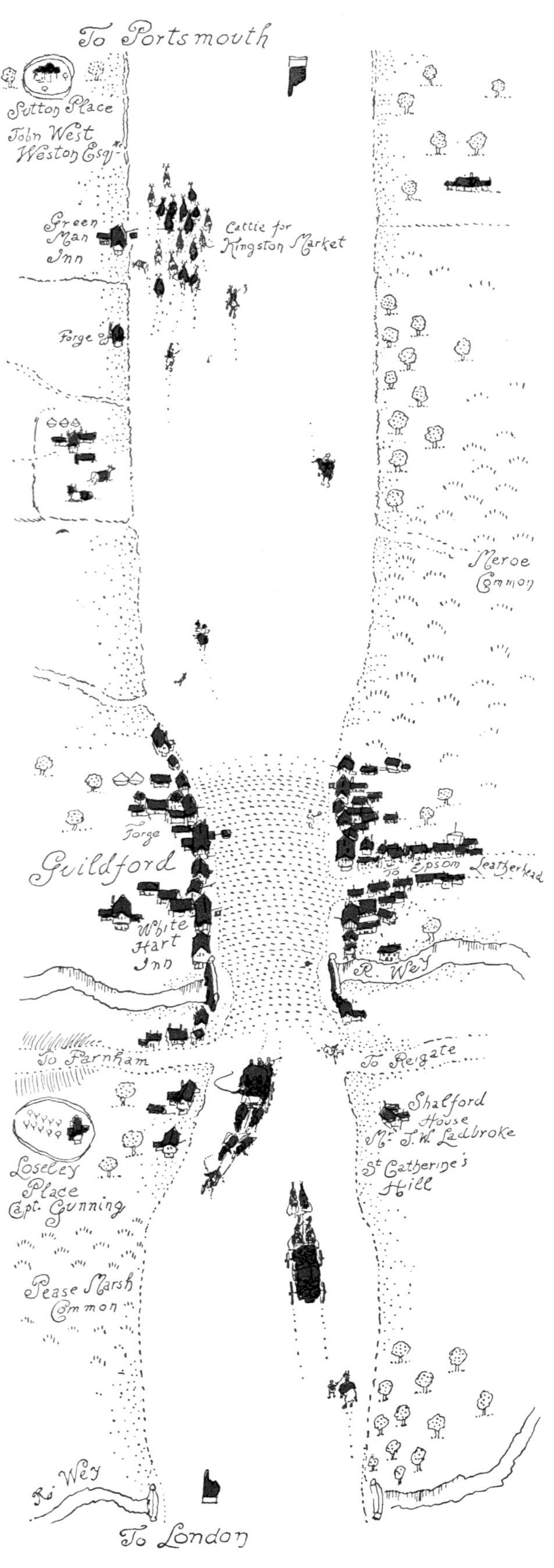

In our times no main road can be so completely obliterated in snowy weather as were the turnpike highways of 1828 when crossing open commons. To-day, telegraph poles almost invariably stand sentinel on them to guide us in the deepest snow-fall, but in the year of our story all trace of the highway in such places would soon be lost.

In those times coachmen and horses—and it was more likely the latter than the former—would have to rely on a sixth sense to guide them; and this is what the "Regulator's" team had to do when travelling this dreary common. An empty coach usually weighed the best part of a ton, and in the heavy going, which was then encountered, horses must have been very hard and fit to draw it the seven or eight mile stages.

A contemporary writer described England as the "purgatory of horses," but one can hardly believe that this was the case.

Thirty years earlier no doubt coach-horses had a very bad time —for there was then no limit by law to their loads, they had longer stages, and a much more frequent use of the thong and the cruel "short tommy." Coaches themselves also were heavier, to say nothing of the coachmen, who always seemed to have run to gargantuan proportions. In those days, the end of the eighteenth and first decade of the nineteenth century, a coachman was chosen more for the power of his arm than for the artistry of his handling of four reins, and there was very little of the refinement of driving four horses which came into vogue after the age of Telford and Macadam. "Nimrod," in the *Sporting Magazine,* tells us that the old rough-and-ready method of getting a heavy coach over the country was not entirely the fault of the drivers—for the whip thong was the only thing that could make four wretched and often half-worn-out horses pull the heavy loads through the axle-deep ruts encountered; and if England was the inferno of horse-flesh of that time, Macadam and Telford were certainly the saviours of the equine race.

In "Nimrod's" time the roads were good; in fact, there were grumbles in the Press of the period that the roads themselves were *too smooth,* and that in consequence there was nothing in the way of jolting to keep sleepy coachmen awake. Thousands of workmen were always employed on these mail-coach roads across England, and the Surveyor of Mail Roads was a very important official.

The same sporting writer told us that it was the pace that killed, and that a mail-coach horse only lasted about three years on fast stages like Hartford Bridge Flats on the Exeter Road, which was almost entirely a galloping one; that a horse in perfectly fit condition might do a six- or seven-mile stage at top speed, but would be very much distressed if taken on a longer stage. Fourteen miles a day was the usual distance for these horses—seven miles on the up and seven miles on the down mails, if enough resting time could be allowed between the two stages.

To horse the mail, proprietors estimated that at least a horse per mile was required, counting both sides of the road.

I cannot think that at the time the "Regulator" travelled the Portsmouth Road England was the horse inferno which it has been called, more especially as, in their own interests, almost all coach proprietors "did" their animals well.

Horses, there is no doubt, were well "done," although on the middle ground and on the night mails some "funny ones" very often had to take their places in the team, "three blind 'uns and a bolter" being quite a usual combination.

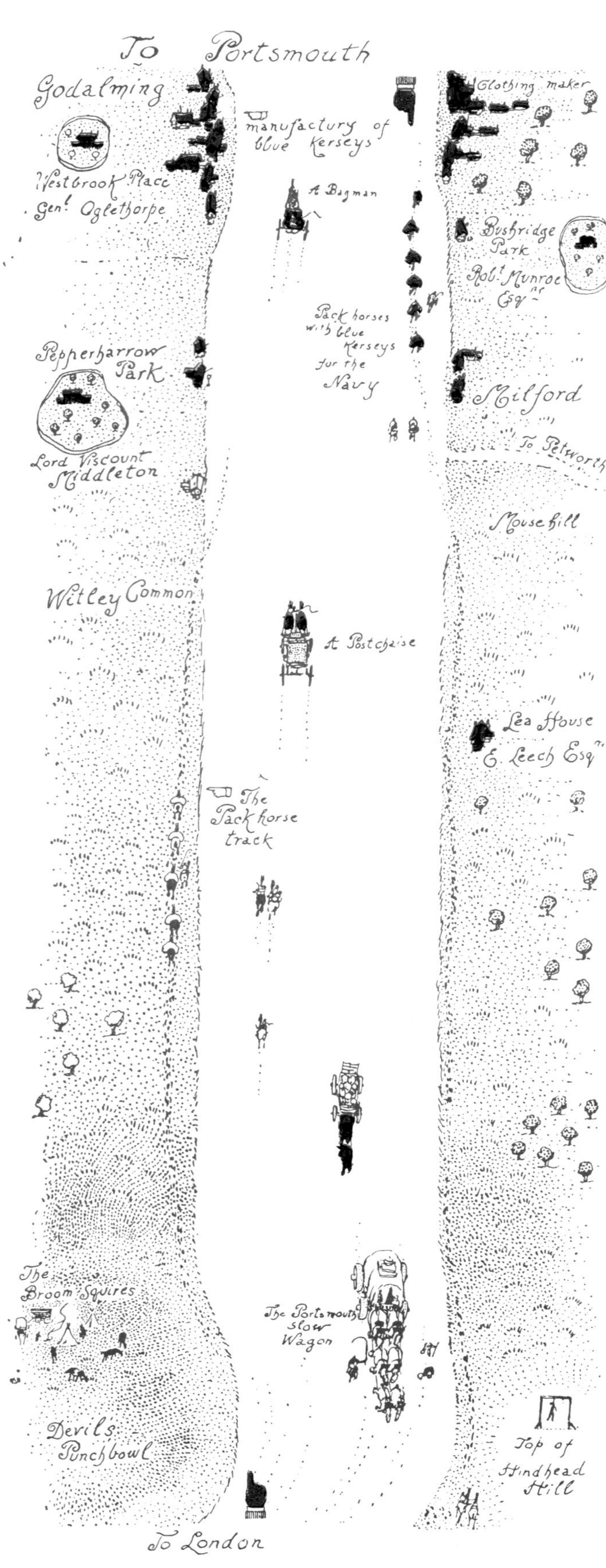

The worst bolter, however, would hardly be able to pull a nineteen-hundredweight coach and its passengers and luggage far by himself.

A coachman on a stage-coach must have discussed many topics with his passengers, and that must be my excuse for leaving the "Regulator" so often on her way to the sea; but while we are talking she is always travelling along the road, and we must imagine that all this time the rattle of her bars and pole-chains can be heard.

Travelling over Wisley Common, Breach Hill, and Oakham Heath, she approached Cobham Gate, nineteen miles five furlongs from the Stone's End in the Borough, from which point the milestones of the Portsmouth Road were measured; past the George Inn at Cobham, where post-horses could be procured, and then swung round by the "White Lion" on her way to Ripley. The King's broad mail-coach highway here stretched away in front of her—an undulating stage which brought her to the Talbot Inn in the village of Ripley, where she made her third change of horses.

But as the coach journeyed quietly over these few miles of undulating and wooded portion of the road, she had passed Pains Hill, where Lady Carhampton was in residence. Although an old woman in 1828 (she died there three years later), in her youth she was one of the most beautiful women of her time. Her gardens were very celebrated, Pains Hill having some of the "finest examples of modern English landscape gardening" (so Pope tells us in 1797). But it was a younger son of the Earl of Abercorn, who was Comptroller of the Green Cloth to the Prince of Wales in 1742, who made these gardens which Pope so admired. The house was afterwards sold to an eccentric individual named Bard Hopkins, who was a relation of the notorious "Vulture" Hopkins, a citizen whose rapacity obtained him the nickname of "Vulture," who lived worthless and died worth £300,000, making a will so that no one could inherit it until the second generation; this, however, was afterwards set aside by the Court of Chancery and the fortune allowed to go to the heir-at-law.

After the eccentric Bard Hopkins's death in 1794, Pains Hill came into the hands of a Scotsman of the name of Moffatt, and subsequently to the Luttrell family; Col. Luttrell (the Colonel of the 6th Dragoon Guards), becoming the Earl of Carhampton, after marrying the beautiful Miss Jane Boyd, the lady I mentioned in the preceding paragraph.

The Talbot Inn at Ripley, where the "Regulator" changed horses, was in 1828 the most important inn in the village; an impressive entrance porch under which the coaches could pull in for the comfort of their passengers in wet weather, and an adjoining cosy-panelled coffee-room whose roaring log fire gave warmth to the cold hands of the "Regulator's" outside passengers, were its chief features. And here full eight minutes were allowed for this change of horses before the coach once more took the road and passed on her way down the long and wide street of the village. Two other houses of hospitality stood on the near side of the street: the George Inn, a picturesque Queen Anne building, but not a posting-house, and at the end of the village, close to the pound and forge, the venerable Anchor Inn, a house much patronized by Portsmouth sailors, by travellers on the broad-wheeled slow wagons, and by drovers and herdsmen.

Between this village and the town of Guildford stood Sutton Place on the off side, across the River Wey, and Clandon Park on the farther side of Merrow or Meroe Common. Sutton Place

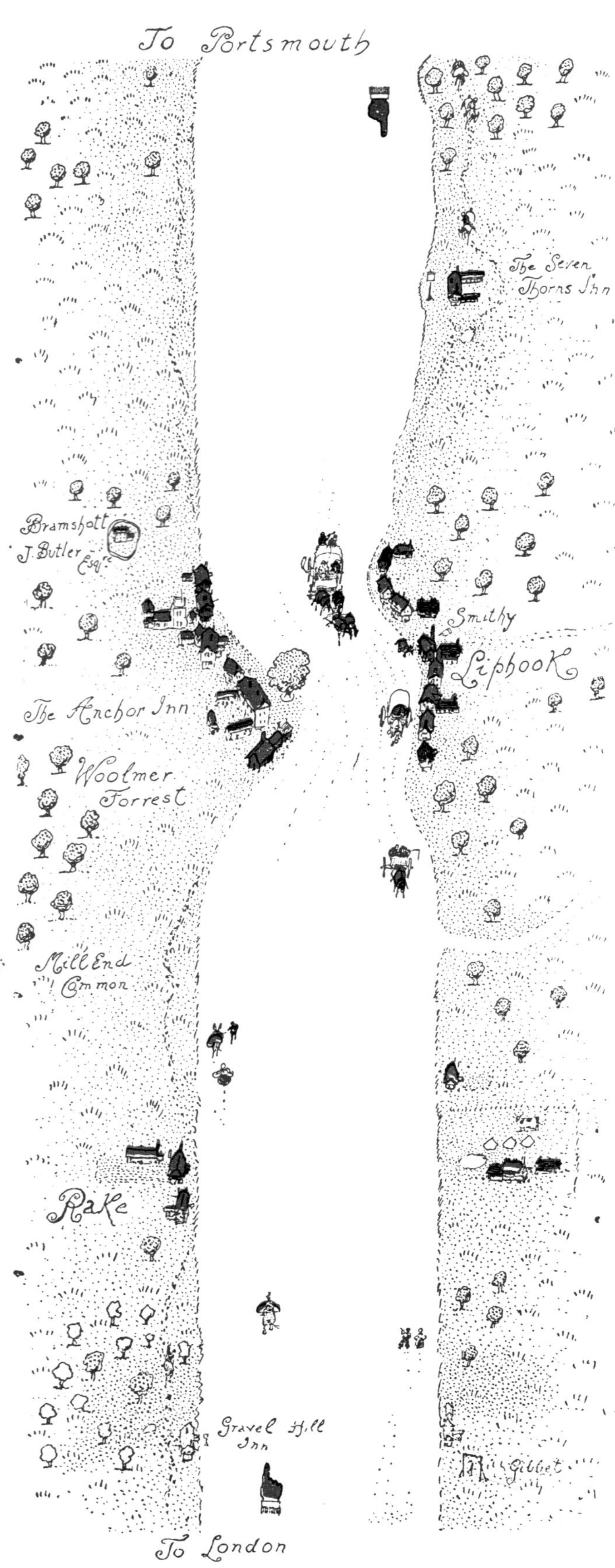

was a very old house which was built for a Sir Richard Weston in Henry VIII's reign. Like most houses built at that time, it originally had a gatehouse tower and enclosed courtyard, but in 1789 the then Mr. Webb Weston had this gatehouse and courtyard removed.

Queen Elizabeth had stayed there in 1591, for Brayley informs us that a letter of the Queen's was dated from Sutton Place in that year, when she wrote to Sir Henry Weston, Kt., her ambassador in France. Her Majesty's stay at the house seems, however, to have brought ill-luck to it, for almost immediately after the departure of her retinue a disastrous fire broke out owing to the enormous fires which had been kept up during her stay (it was in September), and the magnificent gallery, 140 feet long, was completely destroyed.

Clandon Park, on the opposite side of the road to Sutton Place, and some two or more miles away from it, also had its origin at the time of bluff King Hal, a licence to impark the land and free warren being granted to the Weston family, who, after "imparking" and subsequently "disparking" it (according to Brayley), eventually sold it in 1642 to

Sir Richard Onslow of Knole (or Knoll), in the county of Surrey, who again "imparked," "disparked," or "free-warrened" it, "and it has ever since continued to be the principal seat of the Onslow family." This process apparently took time, for it was not until 1731 that the second Earl of Onslow built the house we now see. On the December day in '28 when the "Regulator" passed Clandon Park, the Earl of Onslow was living in a smaller house erected by himself in the village of East Clandon, Clandon Park being empty.

Through the old town of Guildford to the White Hart Inn, its chief posting-house, the "Regulator" slowly travelled. No galloping stage for her on these snow-clogged roads, and very little ease from the incessant collar-work for her struggling teams.

"Little Ease from the Incessant Collar-Work."

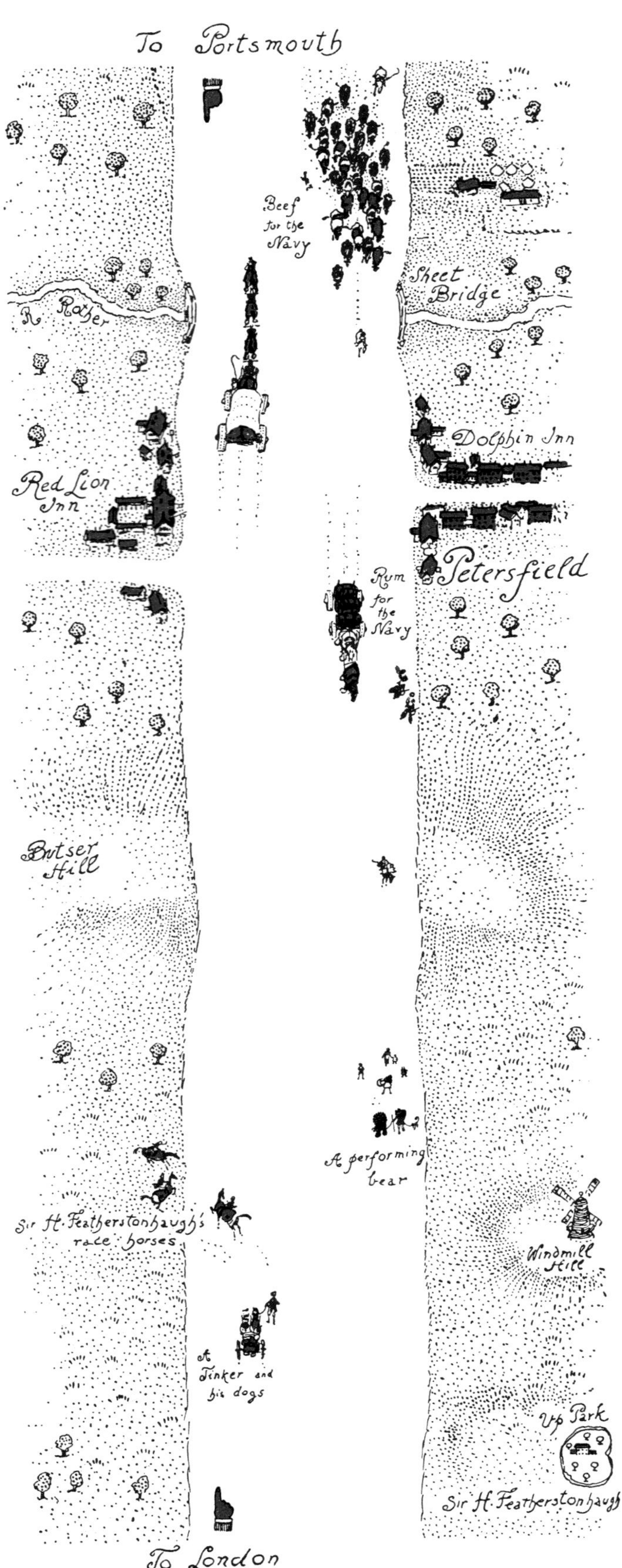

Here at the "White Hart" she came to a standstill for a few minutes, as parcels had to be delivered for the townspeople. A welcome "blow" for the horses before sinking the cobbled High Street, passing over the River Wey at the bottom, and ascending the steep hill out of the town.

Then across Pease Marsh Common, and so to the town of Godalming, where the blue "kerseys" for the Navy were made, and where the fourth change was standing on the road in readiness outside the King's Arms Inn—a long stage, but not quite so long or so tiring a one as that which now faced the waiting team.

But here, as any novice could see, were four horses built more for strength than for speed, for they had the long daily pull to the top of Hindhead, a stage of twelve miles which ran from Godalming to Liphook, and which included the most formidable hill encountered on the Portsmouth Road.

The reason of this long stage was clear, as it was upon this part of the road that the down coach should meet her sister journeying to London, and the teams for this portion of the journey did only one "side of the road," per day, as it was called; they were stabled one night at Liphook, and returned to Godalming on the up " Regulator " the next day, instead of doing the double journey on the same day like the other changes.

A little over twelve miles of road, even on a hilly stage, was not too much for fit horses to undertake, most of the other stages being fourteen miles with a few hours' rest in stables between being taken out of the down mail and " put to " on the up.

What condition these horses must have carried after a month's daily work over this hilly country! What quarters and second thighs they must have developed! I remember, many years ago, when first spending a summer at Porlock, often going to watch the Porlock and Lynton coach come up or down Porlock Hill—by horse-coach being then the only way of getting from the one place to the other. The quarters of the horses in that coach, with its daily journey over some of the biggest hill country in England, were a sight to please the eye of any man interested in horse-flesh; and at that time in the West, who was not?

The way they pulled the loaded coach up Porlock Hill—the undoing of so many motorists—was a lesson in the strength of their propelling hind quarters.

It was a lesson, moreover, which I have never forgotten, and my hunters always go to that country in August for condition.

The "Regulator's" team, which was about to be "put to" at " The King's Arms," at Godalming, while her passengers were partaking of a hasty luncheon, had all of them this big pulling power behind the saddle, but on that day in December '28 a cock-horse had been added, owing to the heavy condition of the snow-covered roads.

Under normal conditions this coach was timed to pass the up-" Regulator " at about 1.45 each day at a point somewhere near the Seven Thorns Inn, on the Liphook side of Hindhead; but on the December day in question both coaches were behind time owing to the snow-fall, and their meeting might quite possibly be in a snow-drift.

Little of the ordinary wheeled traffic of this busy highway had so far been met, and the few travelling post-chaises that had been passed had reported very heavy drifts near the Devil's Punch Bowl.

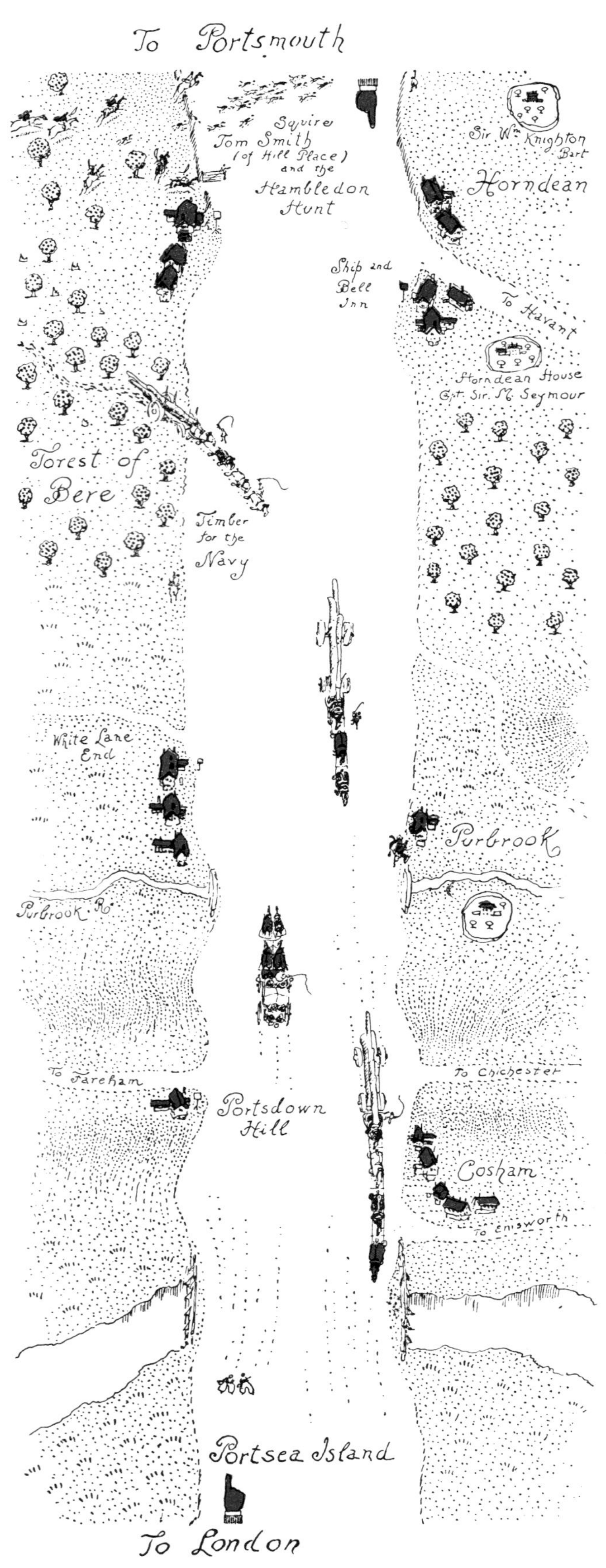

This stage, the wildest and most desolate part of the road, was in bad weather always a very trying one for coachmen, and as more snow had begun to come down the prospect was not very encouraging for the outside passengers or the driver, who would not be sorry to see the end of the stage and the welcome porch of "The Anchor" at Liphook.

It was, however, a consolation for the travellers to know that the "Rocket," leaving London half an hour after the "Regulator," and running to Portsmouth in about the same number of hours, was still behind them, and that both their up coaches should be met somewhere upon this stage, and some comfort to know that if an accident occurred through snow-drifts, help might be available from either direction.

Slowly and steadily the five horses now harnessed in the "Regulator" dragged her through Milford, past the White Lion Inn at Mousehill, over Witley Common by Hammer Ponds, to the long pull upwards to the Devil's Punch Bowl and Hindhead Gibbet.

Seen through the falling snow from the coach top, the ostler's

"To the Long Pull upwards to the Devil's Punch Bowl."

boy astride the cock-horse soon became a grey shadow huddled forward on his mount, only his whip arm moving jerkily up and down, while the steam from the horses rose below these hardy travellers to Portsmouth.

The farther up the rise the "Regulator" travelled, the more the force of the wind, which had been for some time blowing, seemed to increase, driving the snow in whirling masses in front and around the coach, and making it increasingly difficult for her passengers to keep the flakes from descending down the backs of their necks.

Capes were pulled up over heads, mufflers and collars given an extra twist and hoist, as the coach slowly toiled up the hill, while snow-drifts began to accumulate in every hollow and the road itself became almost undiscernible.

Crack! went the post-boy's short whip on ahead. Swish! went the coachman's long thong from the box-seat as he urged his powerful team to further exertions and the coach wheels slowly and silently churned through the ever-deepening snow.

Half-way up the ascent a halt for a few moments to give a "blow" to the steaming horses, and then on and up once more towards the gibbet with its creaking chains on the summit of the Punch Bowl itself.

"In Many Places Deep Worn Ways, Resembling a Devonshire Lane."

Almost at the top the slight banks of snow on either side of the road, which had so far been a guide to the position of the highway, seemed to disappear, and at the same moment there was a cry from the ostler's lad as his horse sank into a drift of wind-blown snow.

As the "Regulator" pulled up, the guard jumped down and struggled forward as best he could to help the post-boy and his plunging lead horse trying to get out of the drift. Having extricated and placed him on a more or less solid foothold, he proceeded to walk by his side and so feel for the turnpike track. Whether or no the coach was still on the highway was impossible to tell, as all signs of its edges had now completely disappeared, and it was only by the position of the gibbet above him that the driver had any idea as to its direction.

On the right-hand side of the coach the ground fell away into the bowl, but in 1828 the highway went right up to the gibbet and not, as it does now, some little way below it.

Then the packhorse tracks each side of it were distinctly marked; in many places deep worn ways, resembling a Devonshire lane.

Through Hindhead Village can still be discovered these hoofways which ran along by the side of the turnpike road; but to-day they pass through private gardens and grounds, the Portsmouth Road now taking a slightly different line.

Below the "Regulator," far down in the Punch Bowl, was a gipsy encampment—a dozen or more tents, a few rough huts, and many shaggy ponies and horses standing in the snow marked the spot where some years before the "broom squires" had taken up their home.

These gipsies were at that time permanent squatters on the land and were the original Hindhead population. Their descendants still own land in the Punch Bowl, and, as original pioneers, have a great contempt for modern Hindhead and its population.

At a later time they strongly resented the encroachments of land speculators and builders on this part of the country, a land which is now becoming so over-built and over-populated that its wildness and beauty will soon completely disappear.

"While the Cock-horse Boy Unhitched His Horse."

A few minutes' " blow " on the summit for the sturdy team, while the cock-horse boy unhitched his horse, and the stage-coach began the run down to Bramshott and the Seven Thorns Inn—an inn which had so bad a reputation at that time that very few of the coaches cared to pull up at it.

Footpads and highwaymen had given it an unsavoury reputation, and road travellers were generally glad when they were safely past its inhospitable doors and neighbourhood.

All this stage of the road was a mass of common and pine woods, and, with the exception of the inn just mentioned, not a house or habitation was passed.

Although on this December day but few post-chaises and travelling chariots had been met, the Portsmouth Road at ordinary times was a very busy highway. All through the day crowds of horse-drawn slow-moving traffic travelled its macadamized surface; for in pre-railway times the turnpike roads of England were very plentifully sprinkled with traffic, and even in winter when snow covered the ground the roads were not entirely deserted. I do not mean that the Portsmouth Road had the Piccadilly Circus appearance that it now has on a Saturday or Sunday afternoon.

I cannot understand why all these people take the trouble to motor from Piccadilly Circus, when they can see just the same effect—the back view of the car in front of them—by motoring round and round

THE ANCHOR INN AT LIPHOOK.

it all day; but there is no doubt that in the year of my story neither the Portsmouth nor any other of our big turnpike roads were ever lonely, but rather they were full of traffic.

What a difference there was, however, to the crowding then and now, when all "Romance of the Road" has disappeared, completely driven off the highway by the rush of pace! In eighteen hundred and twenty-eight the fastest conveyance from London only just got to Portsmouth in a day, whereas now we go down in our car between luncheon and tea and return after dinner; but our ancestors had the mud and dust of macadam in quantities which are unknown to us—mud and dust possibly picturesque, but certainly unpleasant to live with.

No wonder road travellers welcomed the Anchor Inn at Liphook.

"The Picture the Anchor Inn would Make on a Summer Morning."

Although, on that December afternoon, the historic chestnut tree which stands in front of its beautiful Queen Anne façade gave no shelter to lounging idlers, in summer-time it was the meeting-place of the entire village. Under its shade the news of the world was circulated to the inhabitants of Liphook as it was brought into the town by the guards of the London or Portsmouth coaches.

To this tree had the news of Nelson's naval victories been brought by cheering guards, gaily decorated horses and coachmen, a few years before, and in 1827 the inhabitants had "huzza-ed" the be-flagged coaches as they had galloped through the village shouting the news of the Battle of Navarino.

"The News of Nelson's Victories."

"The Anchor," as its name signified, was a naval house, but it had also housed many Royal personages, and its cellars had often held for the night French prisoners of war as they journeyed to London.

On this winter day, "The Anchor" presented a very different appearance to the picture it would make on a summer morning.

Snow a foot deep now covered its roof and the roadway, and while the fresh team were being "put to," the welcome and warmth of its interior were fully appreciated by the coach passengers.

Soon after leaving Liphook the "Regulator's" sister coach on the up-journey to London came in sight, and a short way behind her the "Rocket," also London bound.

Passing another motor-car or, as we sit in a train, flashing by another train is a most uninteresting proceeding—just a crash, a rush of air, and it is over; but meeting a coach-and-four on the road was a very different performance.

As soon as the two guards sighted each other they would blow a welcome; then, very slowly as it would seem to us, the eight horses would converge together, pole-chains rattling, bars a-tingle, until they met, one on each side of the highway.

"HOW THE OLD GREY'S NEAR HIND LEG WAS STANDING."

On this day as the two "Regulators" met, each coachman pulled up to hear from his confrère the news of the road. Warnings as to snow-drifts; where the extra cock-horse was to be found; how the old grey's near hind was standing; or about the new odd-coloured leader for the Horndean team.

Two minutes' pause—a little horsey gossip, a final cryptic "Don't forget Sally" from the up-guard, and the two teams continued their journeys to Portsmouth and London respectively.

Once again the Portsmouth stage struggled on, passing through Rake to Sheet Bridge and then into the town of Petersfield; but, just as she toiled through Rake, the guard pulled out his key bugle and vigorously played "Sally in our Alley."

> Of all the girls that are so sweet,
> There's none like pretty Sally.

From a farm window into which the passengers on the top of the coach were able to see, Sally, the farmer's paralysed daughter, waved welcome to her friend the guard, as she sat propped up in her invalid chair—thanks for this bugle solo, which he played for her each day as the coach passed by. In all weathers Pretty Sally always had her musical entertainment, sometimes one tune, sometimes another, but never was either "Regulator" allowed to pass without giving this poor cripple her daily solo, the one bright spot in her monotonous existence.

"Passing the News."

Many guards and coachmen on the road had friends of this description who perhaps had never been spoken to and yet were known to them as well as many of their own most intimate friends. Oft-times on a journey a coachman's whip-hand would go up to his hat in salute to acquaintances whom he passed daily at the same spot and yet with whom he had never held converse.

Courtesy of the Road —" Romance of the

The Top of Portsdown Hill.

Road"!—to-day it has vanished; but in 1828 we had time for these things—time to recognize our friends and acquaintances as we drove past them, and time to do a kindly act for some poor invalid or cripple if opportunity occurred.

Some of the towns on the Portsmouth Road have made very few alterations in one hundred years, and Petersfield with its market square and old coaching inns is one of them. If we pass through the town to-day, we can see our fellow-passengers of the "Regulator" stage-coach, if we have any romance or imagination, walking its streets; but we, who sit comfortably in our saloon cars, cannot realize the hardihood required to face the hill-tops of the Portsmouth Road on

THE OUTSIDE OF A STAGE-COACH.

the outside of a stage-coach. Ours is an age of luxury in travel; but our ancestors sat on the roof of the "Regulator" from 8 a.m. until 6 p.m. on this winter's day in '28, and if they were "three-bottle men" at the end of the journey they certainly had well earned the right to be so.

At Horndean the last team was put in the coach, and then over the forest of Bere country, past White Lane End to Purbrook House and Portsdown Hill, from the top of which our destination came into full view.

Dropping down to Cosham, the coach rattled over the swing bridge which gave access to Portsea Island and then through Hilsea to "The Fountain Inn at Portsmouth town," and came to the end of her journey.

	Wandsworth	Marquess of Stafford, Melrose Hall Earl Spencer, Wimbledon Park
Thomas Oldfield, Esq., The Fire House Countess de Grey Marchioness of Exeter Lord Gifford Lord Viscount Clifden Earl of Bristol Earl of Bessborough Marchioness of Downshire	Putney Heath	T. Tooke, Esq., Octagon House Earl of Liverpool, Coombe House C. N. Palmer, Esq., Norbiton Place W. Disney, Esq., Elmers F. Robertson, Esq., Woodbines
H.R.H. the Duke of Clarence, Bushy Park	Kingston	
C. Raphael, Esq., Ember Court Lord H. Fitzgerald, Boyle Farm	Thames Ditton	
J. Spicer, Esq., Esher Place Sir E. Nagle, Bart. Sir John Frederick, Bart., Burwood Park Edw. Ball Hughes, Esq., Oatlands Park	Esher	Compton Weekes, Esq., Barwell Court Mrs. Terry, Esher Lodge H.R.H. Prince of Saxe-Coburg, Claremont Park
	Cobham	Countess of Carhampton, Pains Hill H. Coombe, Esq., Cobham Park
John Webb Weston, Esq., Sutton Place	Ripley	Lord King, Ockham Park Earl of Onslow, Clandon Park
C. Spicer, Esq., Stoke Hill Mrs. More Molyneux, St. Catherine's Hill Capt. Gunning Loseley	Guildford	J. W. Ladbrooke, Esq., Shalford House
N. Godbold, Esq., Westwood Place	Godalming	H. Farmer, Esq., Gosden House Lord Grantley, Wonersh
Viscount Middleton, Pepperharrow Park	Mousehill	
Henry Budd, Esq., Foley House	Liphook	C. Taylor, Esq., Holycombe C. Rolls, Esq., Milland House
C. Alderson, Esq., Ashford House Major Boyce, Rose Cottage	Petersfield	General Hugonin, Nursted House Hon. Sir C. Paget, Fair Oak Lodge
Capt. Brydges, The Hermitage	Butser Hill	Sir H. Featherstonhaugh, Up Park
Mrs. Richards, North House Dr. McArthur, Hunton House	Horndean	Sir W. Knighton, Bart., Greenhook Capt. Sir M. Seymour, Horndean House
Col. Conway, The Grove	Purbrook	G. Morant, Esq., Purbrook House
C. Anneslie, Esq., Mount Pleasant	Portsdown Hill	
Thos. Thistlethwayte, Esq., Southwick Park	Hilsea, Portsmouth	J. Burrell, Esq., Stubbington Lodge

EPILOGUE

" Mummy, you know Susan's neck ? "

" Yes, dear, what about it ? "

" W-e-l-l—she's fallen into the pond—up to it," and my book is rather like this little story, because what ought to have come at the beginning is appearing last of all, and your showman is only now introducing to you some of his collaborators.

An Epilogue is but an afterthought, but even now a few lines about the lives of some of these collaborators may not be out of place.

A short time ago at the " Lygon Arms," Broadway, a youth and maiden, while imbibing a cocktail, happened to look at a sketch which was hanging up in the room where your showman also was taking his pre-luncheon *apéritif.*

" It's signed Cecil Aldin," said the youth.

" He must be a very old man now," replied the maiden . . . and, again, a commercial traveller for a persevering publisher once tried to sell to a shopkeeper a print from one of the author's pictures. " Cecil Aldin again," said the prospective buyer; " it's time he was dead."

Notwithstanding these two true (or *too* true, whichever you like) stories, and what must obviously be the patriarchal age of your impresario, he cannot himself remember the Romance of the Road of 1828. His show, therefore, has had to be produced in collaboration with others who lived and flourished at the time. People who saw the Road when there was Romance on it, and not as it is today, " a sink of mechanical toil."

James Pollard, Henry Alken, J. F. Herring, Nimrod, Patterson and many others have kept record of the Romance of the Road of 1828, and to all of these his pen and brush are deeply indebted.

James Roque, Henry Teesdale, John Cary, "map-fellers," have been his assistants in cartography.

JAMES POLLARD.—There was no artist who devoted his work so exclusively to inns, coaches, and the road as Pollard, and for that reason he should come first.

His horses may seem to us a little stiff and conventional in movement, his coaches, to our modern minds, may perhaps be too minute in detail, but to the student of the road every one of Pollard's pictures tells a story, for they are pictures by a coachman and artist combined. Very high artistic merit they may not have, but they hand down to us a story of horses, harness, travellers, mails, guards, and coachmen, which no other limner of the period has been able to do.

I can find no record that James Pollard had ever driven a team himself other than the record he has left in his pictures, but no painter could be so accurate in detail and have so many side-line or by-play coaching incidents in his prints, unless he was an expert at driving a team himself.

Sir Walter Gilbey has recorded that James's father was a Newcastle man, an engraver who came to London in 1782 at the age of twenty-seven, but James, my collaborator, was born in 1797, and was, therefore, thirty-one years of age when my Bath mail and Portsmouth stage-coach journeyed the road.

Seven years before, he had exhibited his picture, "The North Country Mails at the 'Peacock' at Islington," at the Royal Academy and a reproduction of it is included in my book.

He exhibited many other of his paintings of coaching subjects at most of the London galleries, and in later days innumerable reproductions have been made from his work.

He lived to well over sixty-two years of age, but the date of his demise is not definitely known.

HENRY ALKEN was a contemporary of James Pollard, but rather older, being forty-four years of age at the time of my "Romance of the Road." To Alken the world is indebted for some delightful oil-paintings of coaches by moonlight, which, I believe, have never been reproduced as prints.

Today his pictures are more valuable than those of James Pollard, but he made hunting subjects more than coaching pictures his chief work. From what Sir Walter Gilbey says of him in his *Animal Painters*, he seems to have been rather a morose individual, very adverse to any kind of criticism of his own work, and a martinet in his home. An untidy and badly turned-out man himself, yet he always put the smartest of smart men in his hunting pictures.

Henry Alken has not been so big a collaborator as Pollard in this

NORTH COUNTRY MAILS AT "THE PEACOCK," ISLINGTON. (After JAMES POLLARD)

road romance, but he has helped in his pictures to perpetuate the atmosphere of those coaching times.

JOHN F. HERRING, however, is the sporting artist about whose private life we know most, and here was the ideal combination for a painter of coaching pictures, for he was for some time a stage coachman as well as an artist. In 1828 Herring was thirty-three years old, but when he was eighteen he had left his home in Surrey and begun his artistic career by painting animals on the door panels of coaches for coachbuilders, the panels on the doors of the " Reindeer," " White Lion," and " Commander-in-Chief " coaches being painted by him.

Soon after executing these he became the professional coachman on the " Nelson " stage-coach, which ran between Lincoln and Wakefield. At the age of twenty-five, and while still professional coachman on the " Nelson," he exhibited his first picture in the Royal Academy, but later settled down seriously to his art and gave up his driving appointment.

He is known more by his portraits of winners of the classic races and agricultural horse subjects than by his coaching pictures, but when we see a stage-coach painted by him we know that not a buckle or terret is misplaced.

He lived until he was seventy years of age.

"NIMROD" (J. C. Apperley), another of my collaborators, was the great sporting writer of 1828, and his articles in the *Sporting Magazine* and essay on " The Road," as it was at that time—which has so often been reprinted—has helped considerably in the production of this peep-show.

PATTERSON and CARY rendered aid with their road books; and to Henry Teesdale, for his wonderful maps of the roads in 1828, my generous thanks are due. Even today his " English Atlas," published in 1828, always travels with me when on a motor journey, because it is so much more clear and distinct than any maps ever published since.

When our forefathers travelled they either carried the bulky Patterson or one of Cary's "High Roads," which were made in more portable form.

These strip maps were on separate sheets on a scale of one inch to the mile, and kept folded up in a neat leather case.

They gave every "gentleman's seat situate on," or "seen from" the road, the chief inns, and the different turnpike gates, with particulars as to the trusts. A few pages of Cary's strip map of 1799 will be interesting to study and are reproduced in the concluding pages of this volume. They show us who lived near the highway, and give a very clear idea of the small number of houses then to be seen.

Although the originals of these maps were made twenty-eight years before our journeys they show very clearly the number of toll gates at which we then had to pay toll; but we must remember that when my little coaches went on their journeys a very large number of these pikes had been done away with.

Map A shows all these trusts around London and the gates they controlled, and the subsequent maps give us a clear picture of some portions of the roads we travelled over as they were a few years previously.

Just in the same way as the coaches dawdled across the countryside so we could dawdle on, but the coachman must now raise his hat to you for the last time:

"Ladies and Gentlemen, I leave you here,"

and your showman must move on to another pitch.

CARY'S

Survey of the High Roads

FROM

LONDON

TO

Hampton Court,
Bagshot,
Oakingham,
Binfield,
Windsor,
Maidenhead,
High Wycombe,
Amersham,
Rickmansworth.
Tring,
S.t Albans,
Welwyn,
Hertford,
Ware,
Bishops Stortford,
Chipping Ongar,
Chelmsford,
Gravesend,
Rochester,
Maidstone,
Tunbridge Wells,
East Grinsted,
Ryegate,
Dorking,
Guildford,
Richmond.

On a Scale of one Inch to a Mile;

WHEREIN

Every GENTLEMAN'S SEAT, *situate on, or seen from the*

ROAD,

(however distant) are laid down, with the Name of the Possessor,

to which is added

The Number of INNS on each separate Route;

ALSO,

The different ***TURNPIKE GATES***, *shewing*

The Connection which one trust has with

another.

London: *Printed for* J. Cary, *Engraver & Map seller, the corner of Arundel Street, Strand.*

July 1.st 1799.

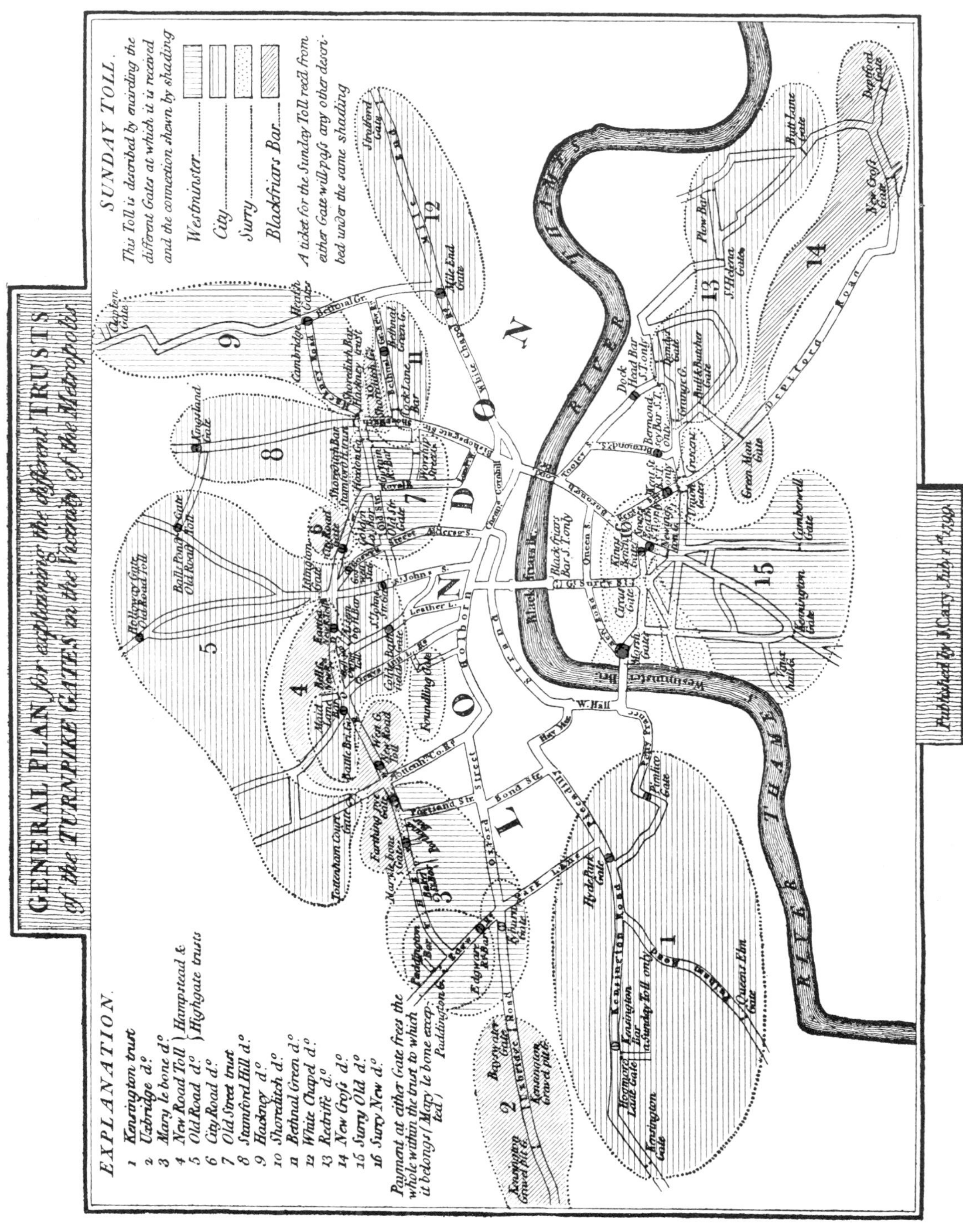
GENERAL PLAN for explaining the different TRUSTS of the TURNPIKE GATES in the Vicinity of the Metropolis
EXPLANATION
1 Kensington trust
2 Uxbridge d°
3 Mary le bone d°
4 New Road Toll } Hampstead &
5 Old Road d° } Highgate trusts
6 City Road d°
7 Old Street trust
8 Stamford Hill d°
9 Hackney d°
10 Shoreditch d°
11 Bethnal Green d°
12 White Chapel d°
13 Rotriffe d°
14 New Cross d°
15 Surry Old d°
16 Surry New d°
Payment at either Gate frees the whole within the trust to which it belongs (Mary le bone excepted)
SUNDAY TOLL
This Toll is described by encircling the different Gates at which it is received and the connection shown by shading
Westminster
City
Surry
Blackfriars Bar
A ticket for the Sunday Toll recd. from either Gate will pass any other described under the same shading
LONDON
RIVER THAMES
Published by J. Cary July 1st 1790

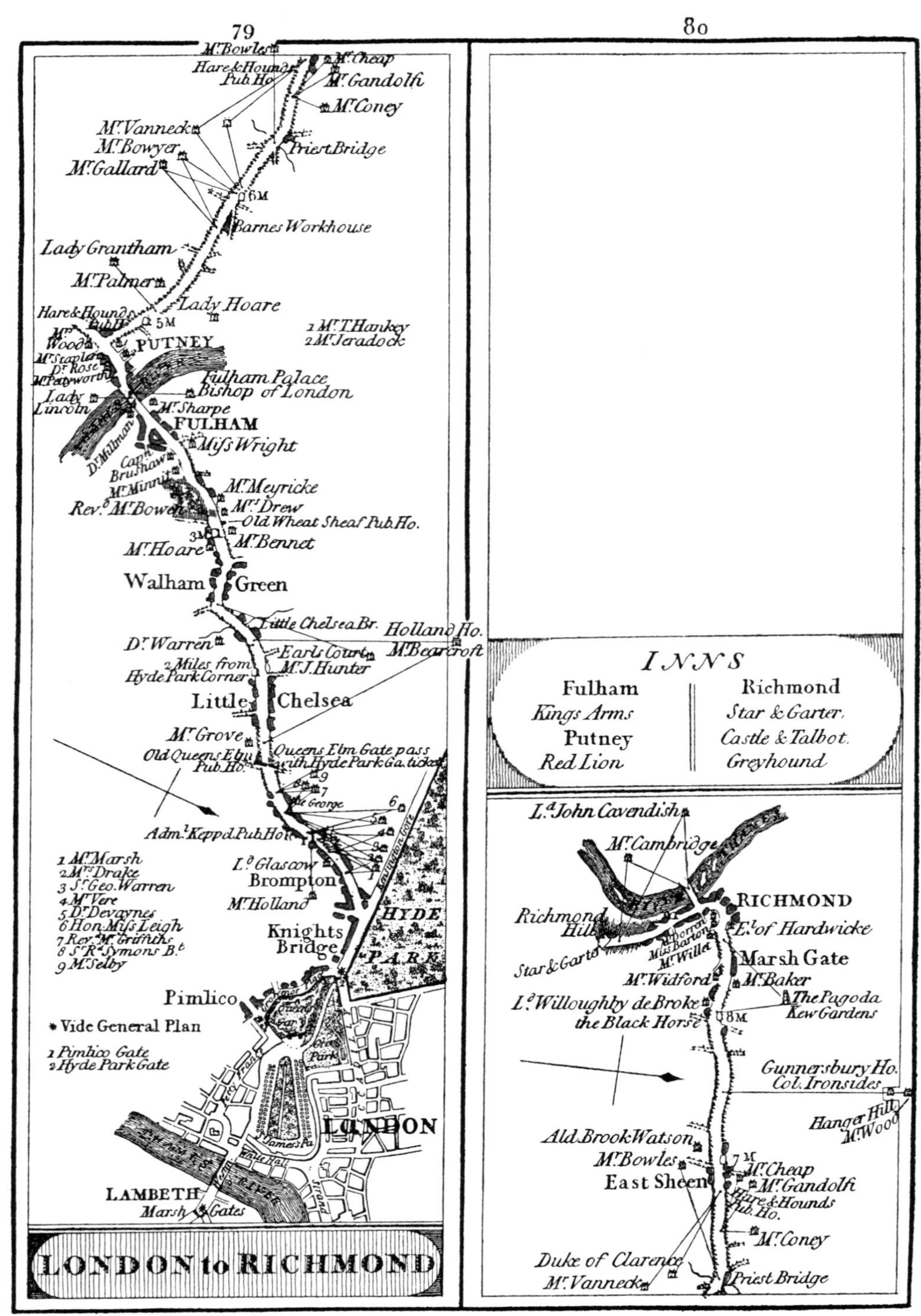
79
80
LONDON to RICHMOND
INNS
Fulham
Kings Arms
Putney
Red Lion
Richmond
Star & Garter.
Castle & Talbot.
Greyhound
RICHMOND
Marsh Gate
East Sheen
PUTNEY
FULHAM
Walham Green
Little Chelsea
Brompton
Knights Bridge
Pimlico
LONDON
LAMBETH
HYDE PARK
* Vide General Plan
1 Pimlico Gate
2 Hyde Park Gate
Published by J. Cary July 1st. 1799.

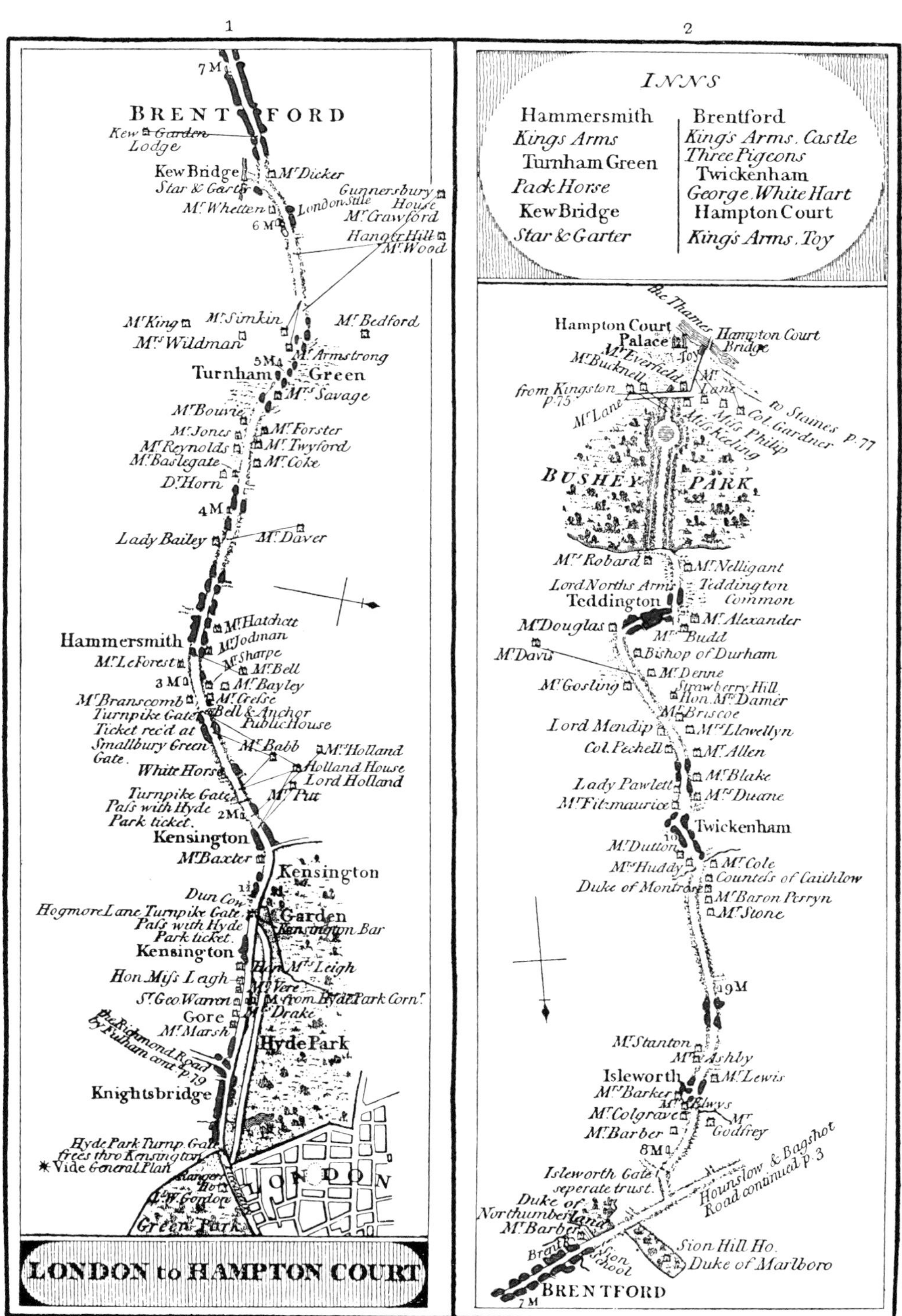

Published by J. Cary July 1st 1799.

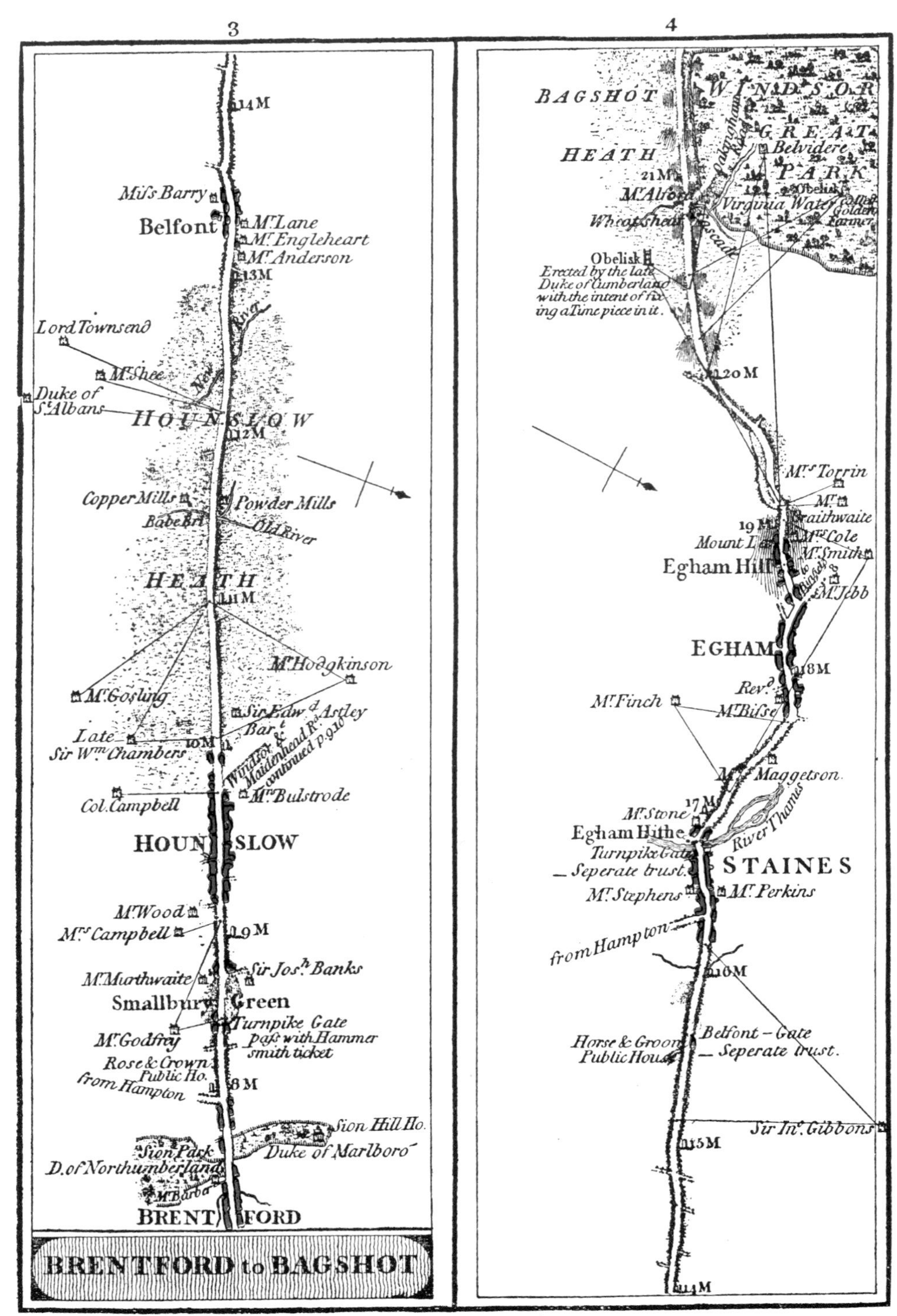

Published by J. Cary July 1st 1799

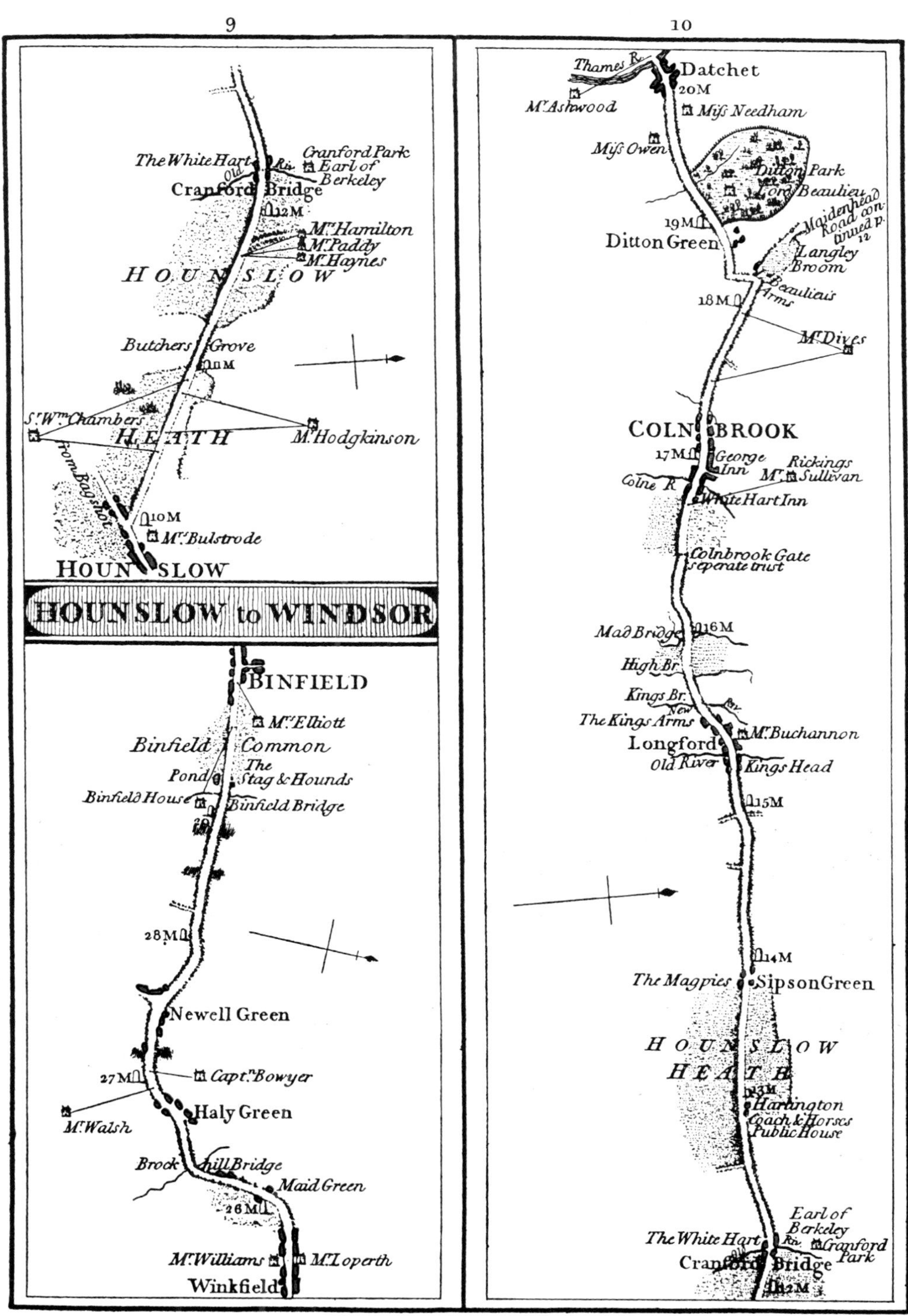

Published by J. Cary July 1st 1799.

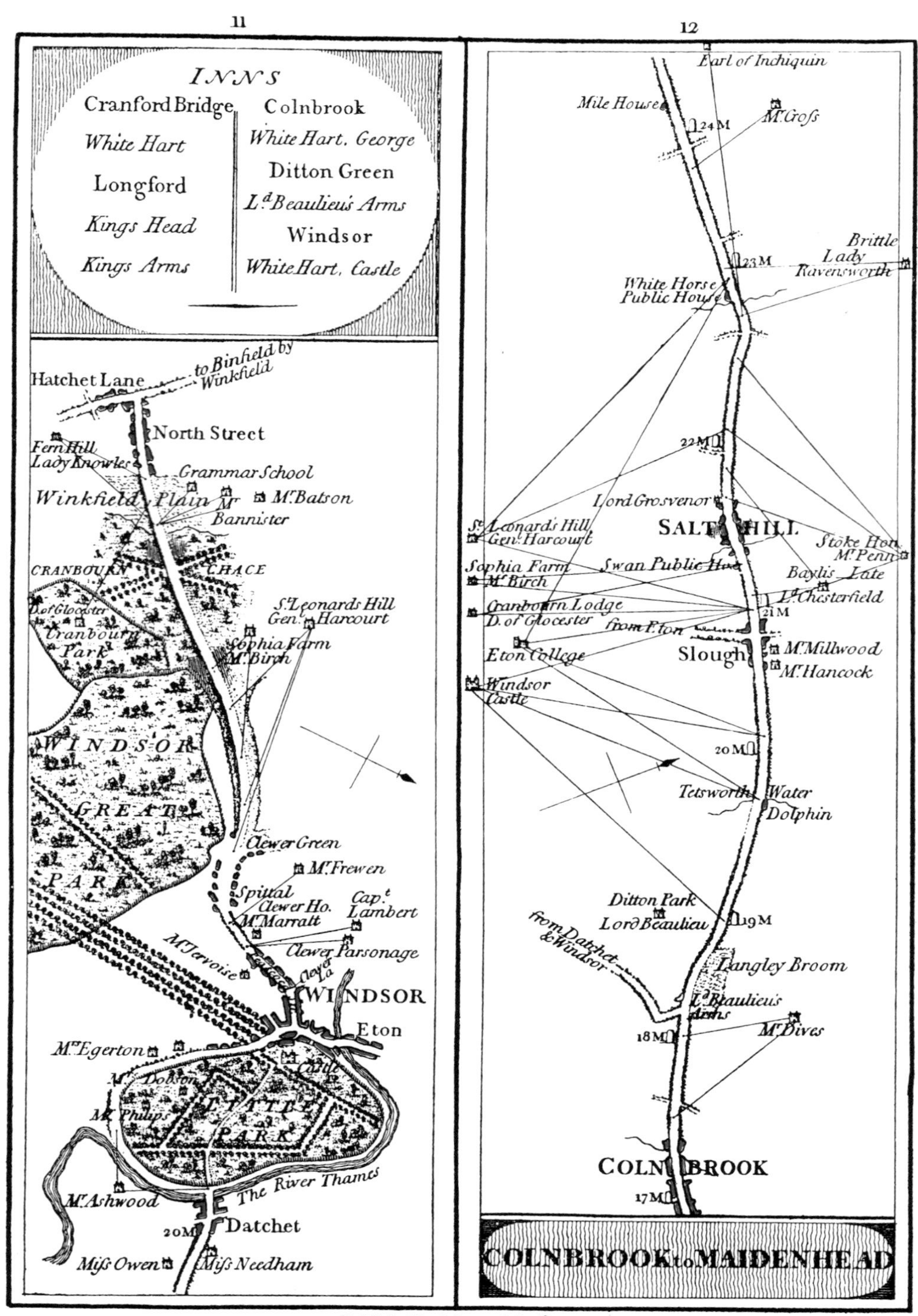
11
12
INNS
Cranford Bridge
White Hart
Longford
Kings Head
Kings Arms
Colnbrook
White Hart, George
Ditton Green
Ld Beaulieu's Arms
Windsor
White Hart, Castle
Hatchet Lane
to Binfield by Winkfield
North Street
Fern Hill
Lady Knowles
Grammar School
Winkfield Plain
Mr Bannister
Mr Batson
CRANBOURN CHACE
St Leonards Hill
Genl Harcourt
Cranbourn Park
Sophia Farm
Mr Birch
WINDSOR GREAT PARK
Clewer Green
Mr Frewen
Spittal
Clewer Ho.
Mr Marratt
Capt Lambert
Clewer Parsonage
Mr Jervoise
WINDSOR
Eton
Mr Egerton
Dobson
Castle
Mr Philips
LITTLE PARK
The River Thames
Mr Ashwood
20M
Datchet
Miss Owen
Miss Needham
Earl of Inchiquin
Mile House
Mr Gross
24M
Brittle
Lady Ravensworth
23M
White Horse Public House
22M
Lord Grosvenor
SALT HILL
St Leonards Hill
Genl Harcourt
Stoke Ho.
Mr Penn
Sophia Farm
Mr Birch
Swan Public Ho.
Baylis Late
Ld Chesterfield
Cranbourn Lodge
D. of Glocester
from Eton
21M
Eton College
Slough
Mr Millwood
Mr Hancock
Windsor Castle
20M
Tetsworth Water
Dolphin
Ditton Park
Lord Beaulieu
19M
from Datchet & Windsor
Langley Broom
Ld Beaulieu's Arms
18M
Mr Dives
COLNBROOK
17M
COLNBROOK to MAIDENHEAD
Published by J. Cary July 1st 1799